Varieties of Unbelief

Varieties of Unbelief

JOHN HABGOOD

DARTON·LONGMAN + TODD

First published in 2000 by
Darton, Longman and Todd Ltd
1 Spencer Court
140–142 Wandsworth High Street
London SW18 4JJ

ISBN 0–232–52320–7

A catalogue record for this book is available from the British Library.

Phototypeset by Intype London Ltd
Printed and bound in Great Britain by
Redwood Books, Trowbridge, Wiltshire

Contents

Preface

The Revd John Bampton, sometime Canon of Salisbury, who died in 1751, endowed 'Eight Divinity Lecture Sermons' to be delivered in the University of Oxford. He stipulated that they were to be preached 'upon either of the following subjects: to confirm and establish the Christian faith, and to confute all heretics and schismatics – upon the divine authority of the Holy Scriptures – upon the authority of the writings of the primitive Fathers, as to the Faith and Practice of the primitive Church – upon the Divinity of our Lord and Saviour Jesus Christ – upon the Divinity of the Holy Ghost – upon the Articles of the Christian Faith, as comprehended in the Apostles' and Nicene Creeds.'

It is a tribute to his foresight and generosity that nearly 250 years later Bampton Lectures are still being delivered, and that many major theological works owe their origin to him. To be included within this distinguished succession was a totally unexpected honour for one who has been outside the field of professional theology for more than quarter of a century. I am grateful to the university electors who took the risk of appointing me, and to the faithful congregation who stuck with the lectures as they were delivered on Sunday mornings in the very formal circumstances of the university church.

A modern bishop or archbishop has little time for the long-term and detailed study which serious academic theology requires. On the other hand, the nature of his work as a bridge-builder across many different social and intellectual divides, and the opportunities this provides to encounter many different types of expertise and points of view, can sometimes make up in breadth what is lacking in depth. That, at least, is my excuse for tackling so large and diffuse a subject as varieties of unbelief.

In some respects it could be said that there are as many ways of believing or not believing as there are people. What people actually believe, as opposed to what they say or think they believe, is highly personal, and more often than not is strongly coloured by individual experience. Rather than examine the standard textbook arguments, therefore, I have tried wherever possible to relate the discussion to particular individuals, or to particular expressions of unbelief, where these seem to me characteristic of a broader constituency. My aim has been to enter into the minds of some general types of unbelievers, and then to indicate in a similarly broad fashion why such unbelief can seem compelling, and why I hold it to be mistaken. Inevitably the choice and the descriptions must reflect a rather personal view about which claims to unbelief need to be taken seriously, and hence require an answer. The lectures can thus be seen as part of a ˙personal pilgrimage, a reflection on the kind of issues I have most frequently encountered, and which have pressed on me most heavily. They mostly concern fundamental attitudes and assumptions which throw doubt on belief in God, rather than difficulties which may arise in believing particular Christian doctrines.

The book is, therefore, in no sense comprehensive, but I have endeavoured to give it some shape by relating it where possible to William James's classic *The Varieties of Religious Experience*. My emphasis on James is also a pointer to the fact that I am not concerned primarily with philosophical or theological arguments, but with the feelings, experiences and cultural influences which tend to tip belief or unbelief in one direction or another.

The lecture format imposes its own constraints as regards style, length and continuity. Rather than rewrite the lectures for publication, I have left them more or less as they were delivered and have included some additional, illustrative material in footnotes, as well as some guidance for those readers to whom ideas and authors mentioned in the text may be unfamiliar. I have also added a few notes to support ideas and arguments which could not be developed properly in the lectures themselves without losing the thread or over-running the time limit.

It remains for me to thank those authors and publishers who have allowed me to quote extracts from the following books: Edward Arnold from E. M. Forster's *Two Cheers for Democracy*, 1951; Blackwell Publishers from Anthony Giddens's *Modernity and Self-Identity*, 1991 and Paul Ricoeur's *Critique and Conviction*, 1998; Cambridge University Press from Charles Taylor's *Sources of the Self*, 1989; Faber and Faber from George Steiner's *No Passion Spent*, 1996; Harvard University Press from Kenneth Gergen's *Realities and Relationship*, 1994; Macmillan from R. S. Thomas's *Later Poems 1983*; Oxford University Press from T. V. Morris's *God and the Philosophers*, 1994; Pantheon Books from Paul Rabinow's *The Foucault Reader*, 1984; Penguin UK from Anthony Stevens's *Ariadne's Clue*, 1998; Profile Books from Alan Sokal and Jean Bricmont's *Intellectual Impostures*, 1998; Random House from Iris Murdoch's *Metaphysics as a Guide to Morals*; Routledge from Akbar Ahmed's *Postmodernism and Islam*, 1992 and Philip Blond's *Post-Secular Philosophy*, 1998; SCM Press from Daphne Hampson's *After Christianity*, 1996 and Don Cupitt's *After All*, 1994; Sheil Land Associates Ltd from Monica Furlong's *Travelling In*, 1971; SPCK from Fergus Kerr's *Immortal Longings*, 1997; Yale University Press from Camille Paglia's *Sexual Personae*, 1990.

I would also like to thank my friend and colleague Raymond Barker for much helpful advice, and those Heads of Houses who entertained me so hospitably during my regular visits to Oxford to deliver the lectures.

Finally, a word of thanks to the unknown sculptors of medieval gargoyles, who demonstrated how faith needs to include a spirit of criticism.

1

Belief and Unbelief

A Bampton lecturer is among other things required 'to confirm and establish the Christian Faith, and to confute all heretics and schismatics.' This is an ambitious task. And the title I have given these lectures, 'Varieties of Unbelief', might seem equally ambitious. So let me start with a disclaimer: my aim is not so much to confute as to explore; not so much to argue with unbelief as to understand it, in the expectation that understanding may draw out some of its sting. My concern is with the roots of religious belief and unbelief, rather than with particular doctrines.

However, since unbelief is parasitic upon belief, in the obvious sense that where there are no beliefs there can be no unbelief, merely an absence of belief, any exploration of unbelief must include some discussion of particular beliefs rejected, not just belief in general. President Eisenhower, addressing an Anglican Congress in 1954, declared that 'the goal should be nothing short of inviting every single person, in every single country in the world, who believes in the power of a Supreme Being, to join in a mighty, simultaneous, intense act of faith.' His Secretary of State, perplexed by the politics of the Middle East, called on Muslims and Jews 'to work together in a spirit of Christian charity'. Both were ridiculed. Undifferentiated faith is not a real option. There can nevertheless be a culture of faith, just as there can be a culture of scepticism, and it is some of the reasons for the shift from one to the other that form the subject of this book.

The shift has not been complete, however. G. K. Chesterton's oft-quoted remark has proved all too true: 'When a man ceases to believe in God he does not believe in nothing. He believes in anything.' It is mostly the mainstream religious faiths which have suffered from the growth of scepticism, a fact which suggests that it is partly the rejection of tradition and convention which have contributed to the change of culture, rather than a rejection of belief in what is now vaguely called 'spirituality'. The International Festival of Mind, Body and Spirit, is a rich resource of alternatives. Denise, for example, 'draws on her Cherokee Indian heritage . . . and is an internationally acclaimed expert in the field of energy medicine . . . her past-lives workshops have allowed many to release their negative programming.' She is also well acquainted with angels, and for a mere £5 will enable participants to 'meet their personal Angel in a beautiful guided meditation. Miracles have happened during this workshop!' Jill 'has researched the science and mysticism of sound with masters from worldwide traditional cultures' and can introduce us to 'the ancient magic of Mongolian overtone chanting'. Theolyn has an extraordinary alphabet said to date back to King Solomon, and also 'had an encounter with an archangel in 1974'.[1]

My intention is not to mock, but to illustrate. A sceptical culture provokes its own counter-reaction, but it is a counter-reaction which lacks the depth and stability of what has been dismissed. A recent American commentator has referred to what he calls 'easy transcendence scenarios', half-acknowledged forms of wish fulfilment which, he says, testify to the absence of plausible hope for many of his fellow countrymen. 'The fact that the devotees of easy transcendence – the self-help programmes, the spiritual journeys, the New Age philosophies – move so rapidly from one to another, as though an endless carousel . . . were forever turning . . . suggests the despair that often underlies the current quest for self-renovation.'[2] Believing 'anything' (in Chesterton's sense) is a pathological form of belief, a hyperactivity when there seems to be nothing more substantial with which to engage. Rather than disproving the culture of unbelief, it can be seen as a symptom of it.

Nearer the heart of my theme is an incident recounted by a

correspondent in *The Times*, who grew up scornful of religion but gradually found faith, after having been bowled over by the experience of beauty. When meeting a former friend in Hyde Park she happened to mention spirituality, and was embarrassed by the look of consternation on his face. 'Catherine, have you become religious?' She sensed that he would have been less shocked at the possibility that she had become a prostitute or a drug addict. She asked herself, 'How, as a society, did we lose our belief and respect for religion to such an extent that it has become social suicide even to mention God?'[3]

Before dismissing that remark as no more than a trivial example of London cultural snobbery, in which social suicide is worse than death, it is worth checking whether this comment by an American philosophy lecturer, on his own experience in academia, might find an echo in universities nearer home. 'What was especially intolerable,' he wrote, 'was the . . . absolutely unexamined assumption that, because I was a member of the academic community, I would, of course, regard sneering at God and the church as meet, right and even my bounden duty.' He went on to describe himself as 'simply revolted by the malevolent, self-satisfied stupidity of the attacks on Christianity that proceeded from . . . "the great secular consensus" ', by which he meant 'just about everyone connected with the universities, journalism, the literary and artistic intelligensia, and the entertainment industry.'[4]

In this country one has only to look at the way in which most journalists, and virtually all headline writers, adopt a tongue-in-cheek approach to the Christian faith, as if to distance themselves from any suspicion of serious concern. I recently came across an extraordinary example in *New Scientist*, where a generally favourable review of a serious philosophical book on science and religion was illustrated, quite gratuitously, with a picture of the Ku-Klux-Klan.[5] The editor seemed to be warning readers against seduction by reminding them of the dark side of religion.

Most people in Britain, if we are to trust the opinion polls, still say that they believe in God. It is clear, though, that the social supports of religious belief, and the visible expressions of it, are slowly being eroded, though at different rates in the four parts of the United Kingdom. Where there is a strong social need to affirm a corporate identity, religion is a favoured means of filling the gap. Where there is no such identity crisis, there has been a steady progression towards the view that religious commitment should be regarded as a purely personal and individual matter. This has consequences for society as a whole, but it also has consequences for belief. Even in an individualistic environment, what people believe, how they put it into practice and how fervently they hold it, depend to a considerable extent on the reinforcement they receive from those around them.

In my first sermon as Archbishop of York, sixteen years ago, I preached on the text from Psalm 11, 'If the foundations are destroyed, what can the just man do?' The sermon was delivered at a time when the churches were under severe criticism from politicians concerning their social role, and because it is relevant to my theme, it is worth quoting a few sentences from it. 'Public faith', I said, 'is about foundations; it is about the things which bind us together, and the values we share, and the goals we pursue. The psalmist refuses to separate this concern with foundations from individual personal goodness and faith. "What shall the just man do?" Of course, sometimes there has to be a separation. Sometimes the most shining examples of personal faith are found just where the going is hardest and public opposition to religion most intense. But most of us for most of the time depend far more than we care to admit on some kind of public validation of the things which matter to us. We don't just want to be individuals. We want to belong to a society which helps us to be what, at our deepest and best, we know we ought to be.'[6] In my subsequent ministry I spent much time trying to explain in a wide variety of contexts that, in so far as a secular society must depend on the moral quality of its citizens, it cannot afford to ignore, denigrate or undermine the very bodies which are most concerned with moral integrity and quality of life.

At the public level the social role of religion has radically altered within a century. We have witnessed the coming to fruition of

4

changes which were in the making long before. Our culture has moved from one in which public religious belief was the norm, to one in which it is now the exception. Looking back over a longer period one can see cultures in which religion was, and in some parts of the world still is, the primary determinant of the life of the whole of society, and unbelief was a capital offence. Religion was the matrix out of which culture grew. So why has it been displaced? And were there good reasons for this? And if there still are good reasons, are they sufficient to invalidate Christian belief itself, rather than some of the social and intellectual forms in which it has been expressed? These are the questions which underlie the chapters which follow, and I want to try to approach them not primarily as a historical or sociological exercise, but through an analysis of different styles of believing and not believing. Hence the deliberate echo in my title of a classic study, very soon to celebrate its centenary, William James's *The Varieties of Religious Experience*.

James realised that what people say about God and the reasons they give for believing, may be quite different from the way they actually feel about him and experience his presence. Similarly the rational arguments which convinced one generation may seem untenable to its successors. This need not imply any failure of rationality as such, but simply that God is no longer felt to be that kind of God. James instances 'the vast literature of proofs of God's existence drawn from the order of nature, which a century ago seemed so overwhelmingly convincing, [but] today does little more than gather dust in libraries.'[7] Whatever God is, we know that he is not the mere external inventor of what the Victorians called 'contrivances', such as the intricate design of the eye, intended to make manifest his 'glory'. We know, too, that if a God exists he must, in James's words, 'be a more cosmic and tragic personage than that Being'. Likewise many theologians realised that the divine watchmaker, the kingpin of Paley's argument for design, was no longer in business, long before some present-day biologists made the same discovery.

There is an interesting example, not found in James, of the

5

occurrence of profound shifts in meaning in the historical use of the word 'atheist'. It is only in comparatively modern times that people have been willing to call themselves atheists, as the word has shaken itself free from its overtones of immorality and sedition. Up till then religion offered the only generally recognised basis for morality, so the word was almost always used in reference to other people, accusing them of some heinous shortcoming, depending on the god denied, the disloyalty attributed, and the moral degradation assumed. Socrates is the classic example, but the biblical usage is very similar. In Psalm 53, for instance, the accusation 'The fool has said in his heart "There is no God" ' is followed immediately by 'they have all become vile and abominable in their wickedness, there is not one that does good.'

It is not surprising therefore that words like 'secularist' and 'agnostic' were preferred among the honest doubters of the late nineteenth century. From the Enlightenment to the beginning of the twentieth century self-designated atheists were a tiny elite. By the turn of the century the implications of the title had begun to change, and there were a few hundred thousand. By the mid-1980s the number was estimated by the *World Christian Encyclopaedia* at some two hundred million, and that does not include the unknown number of those who are simply indifferent to religion. It is difficult to discern how far the rise in these figures represents a general and rapid change in feeling about the presence or relevance of God, or how far social change had simply legitimated feelings which up till then had been kept under the counter, thereby giving a new acceptability to the concept of atheism. What seems clear, though, is that all these people did not suddenly argue themselves into disbelieving.

James may further help us through his famous distinction between different temperaments in their response to religious experience. One can still recognise what he called 'healthy-minded' believers: people whose outlook on life is basically optimistic, who enjoy a rational and undemanding faith, who refuse to be oppressed or depressed by the fact of evil and who seek the best in others. Their gospel is 'become what you are', release

6

the goodness within, live by courage, hope and trust, and put aside 'doubt, fear, worry, and all nervously precautionary states of mind'.[8]

Alongside them are the cheerfully complacent unbelievers, temperamentally similar, but dispensing with a God who is no longer felt to be needed as the guarantor of social and moral values. Here is one of them as quoted by James: 'The men who do not go to church or have any religious convictions are the best. Praying, singing of hymns, and sermons are pernicious – they teach us to rely on some supernatural power when we ought to rely on ourselves . . . The God-idea was begotten in ignorance, fear and a general lack of knowledge of Nature . . . All my thoughts and cogitations have been of a healthy and cheerful kind, for instead of doubts and fears I see things as they are, for I endeavour to adjust myself to my environment.'[9]

We shall meet his kind again in later chapters and in more sophisticated forms – even in the highly sophisticated religions (or is it irreligions?) of those whose god is acknowledged to be no more than a mental construction. It seems to me that believers of this latter kind have somewhat disreputable predecessors in the so-called 'mind cure' faiths of James's day, whose basic thrust might be summed up as 'thinking makes it so'. Many who call themselves agnostics also share what is in effect a complacent form of unbelief – not in their case outright rejection, but a feeling that these are matters which can safely be left on one side.

By contrast there are what James calls sick or divided souls, people who suffer from a sense of meaninglessness and who crave for God, who plumb the depths of despair and who need strong, religious remedies. These are the people whose lives go through crises and conversions, the twice-born, those who discover themselves not by thinking good thoughts but by self-surrender. Beside their experience, that of the healthy-minded looks shallow. They are the stuff of which saints are made. They also have their counterparts in those converted to unbelief. In James's words 'the new birth may be away from religion into incredulity; or it may be from moral scrupulosity into freedom and licence; or it may be produced by the irruption into the individual's life of some new stimulus or passion, such as love, ambition, cupidity, revenge, or patriotic ·devotion. In all these instances we have precisely the same psychological form of event – a firmness, stability, and equilibrium succeeding a period of storm and stress and inconsistency.'[10] It is a pattern which covers everybody from the disciple of Nietzsche to the erstwhile fundamentalist who decides to kick over the traces.

I have followed James's analysis, over-simple and outdated though much of it now is, because he was writing at a crucial period when issues of belief and unbelief hung in the balance. By concentrating on different temperamental approaches to such issues, he can help us to see that the contrast is not so much between feeling and reason, as between different kinds and qualities of experience trying to make sense of themselves.

The phenomenon of unbelief, like belief itself, belongs within a total pattern of life, in which evidence and arguments have their proper place, but are not the only relevant factors. In addition, just as some people are more deeply concerned about questions of belief than others, so some are more naturally trusting and others more naturally sceptical. The underlying causes of different religious attitudes are thus complex and ill-defined. My hope is that by looking at some fairly typical patterns of unbelief it may be possible to go beyond the familiar, and often sterile, arguments towards greater mutual understanding.

The key point, as I see it, is that both belief and scepticism are necessary components of any serious thinking. The unexamined life, we are told, is not worth living. Our unique capacity as human beings is to be self-reflective. We know, but we also know that we know, and are therefore capable of questioning our knowing. The great discovery which undergirds the whole of Western civilisation, from classical Greece onwards, is that only by questioning can we grow in wisdom and knowledge.

At first sight such a claim might seem to run counter to the whole thrust of biblical religion with its emphasis on unquestioning faith and obedience. It is certainly true that both Jews and

Christians have often behaved as if questioning were a sin, and have exacted dire penalties on unbelievers. But, curiously, the biblical writers themselves seem to have presupposed that beliefs, even fundamental beliefs about God, were revisable. How else are we to account for the continual process of reinterpretation as successive writers worked on the material they had inherited, to give it a new meaning for their own day? There are, of course, specific examples of constructive doubt, as in some of the Psalms and the book of Job. Much more central to the Bible, though, are the changing conceptions of God which arise, for instance, from the experience of Jeremiah in his criticisms and complaints against God, and from the challenges facing Isaiah and his successors to enlarge their horizons as they were swept up into world events. The gulf between God as described in parts of the book of Genesis, and God as described by Isaiah, is huge. Yet both descriptions are recognisable as belonging within the same continuity, through a process of refining and reinterpreting, which only stopped when the words were frozen in a written canonical text.

But this then gave rise to a new kind of questioning, faithful to the text maybe, but determined to extract from it meanings which were believable in the light of more broadly based beliefs about God. There is a famous crux, for instance, in Romans 9 where St Paul seems to be implying that God, in order 'to display his retribution and to make his power known' might have 'tolerated vessels that were objects of retribution due for destruction, precisely in order to make known the full wealth of his glory on vessels that were objects of mercy, prepared from the first for glory.'[11] In other words God chose beforehand who were to be destroyed and who were to be saved in order to demonstrate his mercy in saving the lucky ones. If this were true, most people nowadays would feel that such a God was morally and theologically unbelievable. The energy and ingenuity displayed by commentators in trying to explain the passage is itself evidence that its surface meaning has to be questioned, and that such questioning is a necessary part of being faithful, even in the context of being receptive to the biblical message.

9

Essentially I have been making the same point William James made a century ago. Feelings change. Beliefs flourish and die. The context in which belief has to be exercised is always enlarging and shifting its boundaries. And because beliefs themselves are never fully explicit there is always scope for reinterpretation, changes of emphasis and a process of winnowing in the light of experience.

We can see why this has to be so if we look a little more closely at the nature of belief itself. References to texts and doctrines create the impression that beliefs are essentially mental propositions, which may be true or false, and which are held in the mind in a relatively accessible form. Christianity has obviously strengthened that impression, as far as Christian beliefs are concerned, by its emphasis on creeds and doctrines. In practice these function much more like public rallying points than statements about what individual Christians may have decided to be true or experienced as real. As in most walks of life, people tend to accept a broad area of knowledge as generally reliable and useful, and leave it to the experts to articulate it in a coherent and defensible form. This is probably why opinion polls investigating doctrinal beliefs frequently produce such wildly discordant results, even to the extreme of some people apparently believing in prayer without believing in God.

We get closer to actual beliefs if we think of them as clusters of perceptual and behavioural tendencies.[12] We see and feel things in a particular way because that is the way our beliefs shape us. But it is impossible to discover or articulate the whole of this shaping process, not least because the origins of a substantial part of it are buried deep in our personal and cultural history. Furthermore, the pressure of events constantly puts to the test our habits of mind and routines, and enhances or modifies the experience of living in a particular environment. Part of this process consists of reflection about ourselves, and this is true even of apparently unreflective people. We go over what we have done and experienced. We criticise ourselves. We may feel pleasure, guilt or shame. Our beliefs, in short, are tested by events, tested by ourselves, and tested by external criticism and by an awareness

10

of difference between ourselves and others. The questioning of belief is implicit in the process, whether in the form of articulate controversy, a more honest facing of reality or subtle emotional changes. It is ignored only by those whose minds are already closed and whose articulate beliefs have been sharpened and defined to an extent which allows no further criticism.

The narrowing or closure of the religious mind is in my view one of the more disturbing aberrations of religion. In spelling out why beliefs can never be fully explicit, I have been drawing attention to that element of feeling, that recognition of hidden depths and uncontrolled forces, that inter-relationship with the whole of life and experience, which James brought out into the open. Such unknowns can be dangerous. To think of faith as courageous exploration of continuously unfolding new territory, introduces a disturbing element of risk and uncertainty. Hence the search for intellectual security in rigid intellectual maps and false simplicities. These do not necessarily have to be religious ones. They may just as well be scientific or philosophical or aesthetic. For the moment, however, my focus is on religious security and the sort of devices designed to make belief invulnerable.

James has an example of one of these in his description of pietism. Those who take it to excess, he writes, 'require above all things a simplified world to live in. Variety and confusion are too much for their powers of comfortable adaptation. But whereas your aggressive pietist reaches his unity objectively, by forcibly stamping disorder and divergence out, your retiring pietist reaches his subjectively, leaving disorder in the world at large, but making a smaller world in which he dwells himself and from which he eliminates it altogether. Thus alongside the church militant with its prisons, dragonades and inquisition methods, we have the church *fugient*, as one might call it, with its hermitages, monasteries and sectarian organisations, both churches pursuing the same object – to unify the life and simplify the spectacle presented to the soul.'[13] There is no implication here of anything wrong with simplicity itself. Hard won simplicity can be the highest wisdom. But simplicity as a defence against what otherwise might disturb or disorientate is a sign of mental closure.

There are other ways of becoming invulnerable. In an early study of Islamic fundamentalism there was a revealing description of the social profile of those most attracted to the movement.[14] These were young, predominantly middle-class, often the first in their family to encounter tertiary education and to be faced with new ideas and powerful religious literature. A high proportion were studying scientific or technological disciplines which, according to the study, made them more amenable than those in other walks of life to accepting what they were told, more out of touch with the nuances of traditional teaching and more ready to believe in simple answers to complex questions. There was also a tendency to believe conspiracy theories, allied with a strong sense of injustices done to fellow believers in the past.

There are some obvious resemblances to Western Christian fundamentalism which reinforce the suggestion that the motives underlying this style of belief are not purely theological. The attraction of fundamentalism for those engaged in science and technology is also replicated in the Christian context. It is a mistake to suppose that all scientists are open-minded explorers of all kinds of experience. Science nominally thrives on scepticism, but scientists are just as emotionally vulnerable as anybody else, and may need to find security in asking only the kind of questions to which clear and unequivocal answers are possible. At the opposite pole to fundamentalism there is the highly sophisticated modern method of putting oneself beyond criticism by renouncing all claims to realism. There is also a curious irony in the fact that a culture of scepticism, unlike a culture of belief, may have nothing to rescue it from its own entrenched assumptions. Hence one can sometimes observe the curious phenomenon of a dogmatism of unbelief, and a search for invulnerability, which are just as much the products of a closed mind as their religious counterparts. In some circumstances the closed sceptical mind can be even more dogmatic than the religious mind, and it was this that the American academic I quoted earlier found so oppressive.

One of the symptoms of a closed mind is its reliance on polemic. Michel Foucault, in an interview just before his death, had some strong words on the subject: 'The polemicist . . . proceeds encased in privileges that he possesses in advance and will never agree to question. On principle, he possesses rights authorising him to wage war and making that struggle a just undertaking; the person he confronts is not a partner in the search for the truth, but an adversary, an enemy who is wrong, who is harmful and whose very existence constitutes a threat. For him, then, the game does not consist of recognising this person as a subject having the right to speak, but of abolishing him, as interlocutor, from any possible dialogue; and his final objective will be, not to come as close as possible to a difficult truth, but to bring about the triumph of the just cause he has been manifestly upholding from the beginning. The polemicist relies on a legitimacy that his adversary is by definition denied.'[15]

To acknowledge a continuous dialogue between belief and unbelief is a humbler, more humane and ultimately more fruitful way of proceeding. It need not entail 'being tossed to and fro and carried about by every wind of doctrine'[16] as those who want something firmer to hold on to are apt to complain when faced with the kind of programme I am suggesting. There has to be a firmness of belief as well as a willingness to learn, a coherence as well as a flexibility. The dialogue between belief and unbelief carries no guarantee that misunderstandings will be resolved and new insights gained. There is plenty of scope for the pain of remaining constant as that which one holds dear is humiliated and crucified.

Nor is such constancy in the face of adverse criticism peculiar to religion. The same need to balance firmness and openness, coherence and flexibility, is apparent even in those sciences which pride themselves most on their critical rigour. It is hardly necessary these days to refute T. H. Huxley's famous dictum about a beautiful hypothesis being slain by an ugly fact. It sometimes needs a large accumulation of ugly facts before a promising hypothesis is abandoned, and numerous writers have drawn attention to the extreme difficulty of changing any of the fundamental presuppositions undergirding an area of scientific research once these have become established. I accept that the parallel with religious belief is not exact. For one thing the evidences for religious belief are much less clear-cut and much more difficult to handle than most of the evidence for scientific theories.

My point is simply that there are no non-trivial knowledge claims immune from criticism.[17] Nor, as I shall argue in a later chapter, is there any non-trivial knowledge independent of belief. The culture of belief and the culture of unbelief are both necessary. How these are handled, and how they relate to one another, is of some significance for the character of a society and the quality of its life. But Christians in particular ought not to be worried by the kind of duality I have been attempting to describe. The Christian faith has at its centre, in the cross of Christ, a symbol of contradiction, of brokenness, of rejection. As Paul Tillich once put it, 'That symbol is most adequate which expresses not only the ultimate but its own lack of ultimacy.'[18] Or to translate it back into the kind of terminology I have been using: that way of life is most coherent and resilient which incorporates both belief and unbelief in a story which still has surprises in store for us.

2

A Matter of Proportion

Those who wonder if there is any room for flamboyance among scientists need look no further than Richard Feynman. He was by all accounts a most engaging and extraordinary human being – a brilliant, Nobel Prize winning, theoretical physicist, a compelling lecturer, an accomplished artist, a practical joker who cracked safes for fun in Los Alamos during the atom bomb project, a vigorous bongo drummer, a romantic who married his wife when he knew she was dying, a man who devoted his life to science, not for any high moral purpose but because he loved finding out, and who towards the end of his life captured popular imagination in a series of autobiographical essays full of off-beat humour – a modern Renaissance man.[1]

In a television documentary made not long before his death he disclaimed any idea that scientists are merely cold analysts, unconcerned about the wholeness and beauty of things, insensitive to Wordsworth with his primrose by the river's brim. Quite the contrary. The scientist sees what the poet sees, but also sees more, is interested in more, asks more questions and discovers new kinds of beauty. But the larger questions about what it all means, and what mysteries might underlie it, are probably unanswerable, he said. To discover real answers about the way things fit together, and to appreciate this other level of beauty, it is necessary to go through a hard scientific grind. There are no short cuts, and there are no truths except reproducible truths. The familiar religious stories told to explain our place in the world are too simple, too contradictory and too provincial. They are not in proportion to the actual wonders and complexities of the world as science has disclosed them. Feynman was convinced that it was better to live without worrying about ultimate mysteries.

I see him as an almost archetypal example of the healthy-minded unbeliever. He proved by the very diversity of his interests that a wide range of human feelings and experiences mattered to him. He lived life to the full, but there was no place in his imagination for religion; it was not something which bothered him, or even particularly interested him. In his eyes it was out of proportion.

There are less sympathetic ways of expressing the same idea. An atheistic scientist, who usually has a great deal to say about religion, was asked a few years ago whether the size of the universe made him feel insignificant. He replied emphatically that it did. 'We're just a bit of slime on a planet belonging to one sun. There could be billions of them. There could be other universes. It makes us really, totally insignificant.'[2] In justice I must add that he also described how human beings might possibly be significant if it is the case – which he thought unlikely – that we are unique in our ability to observe the universe. But the word I want to focus on is that word slime. It implies an extraordinary denigration of all that is important to human beings, an awareness of disproportion between ourselves and the universe, which reduces humanity to a kind of contamination, as seen from the god-like perspective of the atheist who really knows the measure of things. It is a revealing admission of what can happen when questions of scale set the tone of our thinking.

Worries about disproportion are by no means a modern phenomenon. Size is only one aspect of it, though it is the one which immediately springs to mind. There is a temptation to exaggerate the extent to which twentieth-century discoveries about the immensity of the universe have altered people's perception of themselves and their place in it.[3] Even in medieval times the universe was thought to be quite large, with a diameter of some 125,000,000 miles. According to Copernicus this should be multiplied by a factor of about 2000. Neither picture gives the impression of snugness. Pascal was describing 'the whole visible

16

world as only an imperceptible atom in the ample bosom of nature',[4] three centuries before anybody knew about galaxies. But he did more than express his terror at 'the eternal silence of these infinite spaces.'[5] He also drew attention to the fact that human beings stand, as it were, at the midpoint in nature, 'a nothing in comparison with the infinite, an all in comparison with nothing, a mean between nothing and everything'[6] or – as we might put it today – tiny before the stars, immense in the organised complexity of our atomic constituents which equal the stars in number. Pascal, like our modern atheist, went on to make his famous remark about man as no more than a fragile reed, but a thinking reed, more noble than the universe in that we can understand it.[7]

None of this has prevented latter-day cosmologists from trying to frighten us with mathematics. I grew up in the period when Sir James Jeans and Sir Arthur Eddington were writing things like: 'We find the universe terrifying because of its vast meaningless distances, terrifying because of its inconceivably long vistas of time which dwarf human history to the twinkling of an eye, terrifying because of our extreme loneliness, and because of the material insignificance of our home in space . . . but above all else, we find the universe terrifying because it appears to be indifferent to life like our own.'[*] This is still the stuff of much popular science, despite pertinent questions about whether small distances are necessarily more meaningful than large ones, whether it makes any sense to worry about being lonely among the stars or belonging within a merely average galaxy, and how we know the universe is indifferent to us when it has plainly brought us into

[*] The absurdity of this kind of statement was devastatingly exposed in Susan Stebbing's *Philosophy and the Physicists* (Dover, 1958). Archbishop Michael Ramsey's elder brother, Frank, was a highly intelligent healthy-minded unbeliever and, until his early death, a close collaborator with Wittgenstein. He once wrote: 'Where I seem to differ from some of my friends is in attaching little importance to physical size. I don't feel the least humble before the vastness of the heavens. The stars may be large, but they cannot think or love; and these are qualities which impress me far more than size does. I take no credit for weighing more than seventeen stone.' (Quoted in J. M. Keynes, *Essays in Biography* (1933), p. 251.)

being. As Pascal saw, it is not a question of absolute size, because size itself is not a moral quality. It is a question of what you use as your measuring stick.

The same is true of time, though in this case the adjustments which had to be made to popular perceptions probably had a greater moral and religious impact than the adjustment to living in a much larger universe. Time horizons only began to expand in the latter half of the eighteenth century, mainly under the influence of geology, and hit popular imagination with the discovery of the dinosaurs. The task of envisaging prehistory, of imagining what the world of the dinosaurs must have been like and the realisation that there must have been aeons of time before humanity appeared, brought home the reality of a world outside the familiar biblical stories, much more powerfully than reflection on the number and distance of the stars.[8] The Christian faith, just because of its reliance on history, has necessarily been more conscious of time than of distance, and Christian history suddenly began to look very short and insignificant. Thus the awareness of a disproportion in time scales needs to be taken that much more seriously, and I shall be returning to the point later.

Meanwhile, I want to bring into the picture other possible reasons why feelings of disproportion may encourage optimistic characters like Feynman, whose work is fulfilling and whose temperaments are untroubled, to live their lives as if religion were of no account. Churches nowadays usually attract widespread public attention only when something goes wrong. In this they are probably not all that different from other serious public institutions. Their increasing marginalisation is a sign that many things officially held to be the most important in life, no longer feel important within the day-to-day interests of ordinary people. This is not just lack of media attention. Activities explicitly labelled 'religious' can seem rather trivial to those engaged in the demanding work of disclosing the secrets of the universe, putting the world to rights, running high-powered businesses or even just making a lot of money. In many people's minds religion appears as no more than a minority interest for those who happen to like that kind of thing. Outside extremist circles it is often felt to lack the creative energy which once made it so pre-eminent. Iris Murdoch put her finger on such perceptions when she wrote: 'Christian theology may well begin to feel that whereas other (for instance scientific) modes of thought in this age are producing new and profoundly revolutionary ideas, its activity is limited to the manipulation of a given number of ageing concepts.'[9]

It is a thought which brings us nearer, I believe, to the heart of what Feynman was saying. He expressed the feeling – and it was a feeling not a thought-out conclusion – that the basis of religion was too restricted, too provincial and not sufficiently amenable to hard intellectual exploration, to carry the weight ascribed to it. It may once have done so, but the world has moved on. Nor is it just the size of the universe or the aeons of time which are disorientating; it is the impact of the huge expansion of intellectual horizons and the sense of limitless possibilities of technical advance. The modern world is swamped by an overload of ideas and information, of which the internet has become the symbol. There is so much of it out there – raw, unlabelled, unassessed and unassimilated. Facts for the sake of facts. Paul Ricoeur has spoken about 'the indefinite multiplication of signs in circulation in our societies, in comparison with the very small number of texts available in the Middle Ages. The small voice of biblical writings is lost in the incredible clamour of all the signals exchanged.'[10] Furthermore the number and variety of these other voices has a levelling effect, in that it becomes more and more problematic to think of any one text as authoritative.

When Feynman used the phrase 'too simple' about religious stories, I suspect that this apparent limitation of subject matter was part of his meaning. The New Testament is a very short book, a mere 200 pages or so, absurdly small and insubstantial in face of the mountains of evidence available within the sciences. The fact that works of scholarship on the New Testament could fill several libraries, only raises the further question of how such a short text can validly sustain so much scholarly effort, and whether the well must inevitably run dry. Can the great central Christian stories and symbols retain their power under such a barrage of criticism, commentary and reinterpretation, not to mention exploitation by those not primarily concerned with their religious meaning? Some Christians worry about the huge weight of scholarship for a different reason. For them it has had the curious effect of limiting access to the New Testament, turning it into a book for experts only, to such an extent that they are nervous about making their own judgements. The text itself seems to have been lost under a welter of learned exposition.

In describing Christian sources as simple and provincial Feynman had a point, but one which should be familiar to theologians. Despite the vast extent of theological learning (and who could doubt its extent in Canon Bampton's own university?), there remains a strong Christian incentive towards a relative simplicity at the heart of faith, reliance on a few fundamental images and insights and the use of these to interpret experienced complexity. And why not? I have myself frequently used the analogy of light. Light may derive from a single source, and in that sense be utterly simple; but it can be reflected back to our eyes in patterns as complex and varied as the world itself. The simplicity of an illuminating insight, far from precluding complexity of understanding, may actually enable it. Darwin could have made the same point. His theory can be expressed in a single sentence, yet seems inexhaustible in its applications.

Feynman's use of the phrase 'too provincial' likewise has echoes in centuries of theological thought. The apparent scandal that a particular time, and a particular place, and a particular people or person, are uniquely significant in the purposes of God, have been both a boast and a problem for Jews and Christians from the very beginning. But the provinciality of the claim has tended to look more stark as other horizons have expanded. Within the history of the universe and amid the multiplicity of possible worlds, the last two thousand years on earth may not seem particularly special – except to us.

I have already linked both phrases – too simple and too provincial – with Iris Murdoch's comment about 'a given number of ageing concepts'. She made it in the context of a discussion about demythologised Christianity and the need for it to recapture the creative power which at one time expressed itself in great art. The fact that not much art these days seems to be inspired by explicitly religious themes may, however, be a reflection of the trivialisation and disorientation of art itself. When we are told by serious critics that the definition of a work of art is that somebody calls it a work of art, it would seem that cultural impoverishment has spread far beyond religion. So is it really true that the wells of Christian inspiration are drying up? It would be strange if this were so because biblical faith is centred on what have always been the foundational experiences of ordinary life – birth and death, suffering and restoration, loving and forgiving, eating and travelling, hoping, striving and discovering one's limitations. It is true, though, that specific biblical imagery no longer resonates for many people, indeed it simply creates obstacles, and they therefore fail to explore the traditional sources of inspiration. Other symbolisms, such as music, literature or even soap operas, have to a limited extent provided alternatives.

Feynman was expressing feelings which I suspect are widespread among what William James called healthy-minded unbelievers, and which have tended to put serious concern with religion out of the reach of many otherwise well-adjusted people. The feelings are reinforced, as they were in him, by the fact that in some parts of the world religion seems to be a major source of conflict, bigotry and intolerance. But for a great many reflective people, the emotional pressures are not all in one direction. It is all very well to be suspicious of simplicity, to discount tradition, to disdain historical rootedness and to dislike churches, but it is hard to escape the residual longing for some kind of transcendence, some sense that life is more than it appears to be. Even the well-adjusted may be uncomfortably aware of whole areas of experience which have hitherto been ignored, especially in the face of what I have called foundational experiences, such as birth and death, suffering, loving and forgiving. It is in such moments that it does not seem so foolish to believe that persons really matter in the scheme of things. And it can make sense to look again at the supposed validity of the assumption that a faith tied to history, and centred on a person, cannot be universally true.

I begin with an obvious point about symbolism, because learning to work with symbols is an essential part of religious perception, as well as a cause for much suspicion among those whose disciplines have taught them to be literal minded. A symbol, unlike a modern logo, cannot be invented; it has to grow. Effective symbols have accumulated clusters of feelings, perceptions and associations within the developing life of a cultural community, and hold these in relation to one another as vehicles for conveying additional meaning. At their simplest they may be just a colourful way of adding emphasis. At their most archetypal they may represent realities which escape exact definition, just as the best poems are untranslatable into prose.

Symbolic communication, by operating at a deep emotional level, can often touch the springs of belief and action far more effectively than rational argument. But the essential point I want to make is that symbols derive their power from their history.★ It may be an immensely long history, stretching back even into prehistory, like the symbolism of light and darkness. Or it may be short, rooted in a particular powerful or tragic event, such as Hiroshima or Auschwitz. Already with Auschwitz, for example, one can see the event accumulating universal overtones from the long history of Jewish persecution and from the problem of suffering in general. Symbols like this focus emotion, they add density to what needs to be expressed and, at their most profound, they provide a language for what is beyond description.

In religion symbols are irreplaceable. Religious language, if it is to work at all, has to be at the very least symbolic, though that

---

★ Wittgenstein constantly made the same point about all language. It belongs within and expresses a form of life with a history. Here in *Culture and Value*, he puts it epigrammatically: 'Esperanto. Our feeling of disgust, when we utter an *invented* word with invented derivative syllables. The word is cold, has no associations and yet plays at "language".' (1998 Edition), Blackwell, p. 60e.

does not preclude it from carrying literal meanings as well.★ The symbolic meanings have to have time to grow. Thus if we try to abstract a religious faith from its history, we lose most of its power. The thin language of bare description can carry none of the emotional and imaginative charge needed to penetrate beneath its surface. If the limits of our language really are the limits of our world, as Wittgenstein insisted, then it is important that we have a rich language, full of overtones and associations, capable of disclosing or hinting at what lies beyond the reach of inventiveness and insight. It follows that all faiths which aspire to this kind of symbolic richness must draw from a treasury of images, stories and sayings which go back to their historical roots. Provinciality in this broad sense is thus an inherent feature of developed religion and the developed consciousness which can go with it. The accusation that it limits imagination misses the point entirely. The historical particularity of a religious faith, drawing on millennia

---

★ Paul Tillich, *Dynamics of Faith* (Allan and Unwin, 1957), p. 45. The most memorable description of a religious symbol irrevocably shaped by its history is Martin Buber's reply to a friend who asked him why he continued to use the word 'God'. 'Yes, it is the most heavy laden of all human words. None has become so soiled, so mutilated. Just for this reason I may not abandon it. Generations of men have laid the burden of their anxious lives upon this word and weighed it to the ground; it lies in the dust and bears their whole burden. The races of men with their religious factions have torn the word to pieces; they have killed for it and died for it, and it bears their fingermarks and their blood. Where might I find a word like it to describe the highest? If I took the purest, most sparkling concept from the inner treasure-chamber of the philosopher, I could only capture thereby an unbinding product of thought. I could not capture the presence of Him whom the hell-tormented and heaven-storming generations of men mean. Certainly they draw caricatures and write "God" underneath; they murder one another and say "in God's name". But when all madness and delusion fall to dust, when they stand over against Him in the loneliest darkness and no longer say "He, He", but rather sigh "Thou", shout "Thou", all of them the one word, and when they then add "God", is it not the real God they implore, the One Living God, the God of the children of men? Is it not He who *hears* them? And just for this reason is it not the word "God", the word of appeal, the word which has become a *name*, consecrated in all human tongues for all times?' *The Eclipse of God* (Scribner, 1952), pp. 7–8.

of experience, provides grounds of exploration and discernment as fertile as any in the natural sciences.

There are, nevertheless, the associated intellectual problems to which I have already referred, and of which theologians and philosophers of religion need no reminding. How can a faith which claims to be the bearer of universal truths be validly rooted in a particular fragment of history, given the contingency of actual historical processes? In Christian terms, how can we claim that Christ is the centre of history when we know so much more than our predecessors about the range, sweep and uncertainty of events in time? Feynman would have had no interest in either Hegel or Kierkegaard, but it is impossible to do justice to the issues at stake in his rejection of the particularity of Judeo-Christian tradition without at least a passing glance at both of them. I want to approach them, however, via an analogy from evolution, which I think he might have found more amenable. It concerns a current dispute within evolutionary biology.

How far is the actual course of evolution dictated simply by a succession of random events, or how far are the contingencies which drive it part of some larger constraining process? Christian apologists have tended towards the latter view, describing evolution as God's way of creating, and postulating the unfolding of a divine purpose within it. It is an interpretation which provokes fury and contempt among those biologists for whom the sheer contingency of evolutionary events precludes all idea of purpose or direction. It is a matter of the merest chance, they say, that this or that life form happened to evolve the way it did. Had conditions been slightly different millions of years ago, there would be no human beings, no intelligent life forms and nobody to ask questions about the meaning of it all. It is clear that we have no special place within the universe, and awareness of the contingency of the whole process should put a stop to all talk of purpose or providence.

On the other hand, there are biologists who are not quite so sure. Is it really the case, for instance, that the evolution of intelligence has been purely fortuitous? It is at least plausible to argue that, in an unpredictable environment, intelligence and responsive-

24

ness are bound to give an evolutionary advantage, and therefore are bound to evolve – not necessarily in the precise form in which we ourselves experience them, but almost inevitably in some form. If this were not plausible, who would bother to look for signs of extra-terrestrial communication? The enormous energy and expenditure devoted to the search rests on the assumption that where there is life there must in the long run be intelligence.

There are further grounds for doubting whether purely contingent events irrevocably set the course for evolution, as if a rivulet flowing down a mountainside were once and for all to determine the course of a river, irrespective of the geography of the terrain through which it subsequently flows. Evolutionary experiments using colonies of bacteria are beginning to demonstrate how, in the long run, those properties emerge which are best fitted to cope with a particular environment, *whatever the precise history of the colony which is evolving.* In short, while historical events may be contingent, in the end things evolve the way they do at least in part because of their environment and because the world in general is the way it is.[11] There is thus an element of givenness about the whole process, which in no way negates the importance of individual lives and actions, but which defines their context and hence their significance.

This is an analogy, not a theological argument, but it seems to suggest that we do not necessarily have to choose between a process with definable ends on the one hand, and historical contingency on the other. In fact both Hegel and Kierkegaard might have something to teach us.

In Hegel's thought particular events can be representative of the whole because history as a whole has a meaning. It is a rational process of development, an unfolding of a timeless idea, famously summed up in the sentence, 'The history of the world is none other than the progress of the consciousness of freedom.'[12] This is not freedom to act capriciously, however, but freedom to fulfil our natures as rational beings, in other words in accordance with the idea which underlies, and is revealed within, the dialectical and ultimately explicable process of events which we call history.

Nothing is accidental or indifferent, and the particular events of the Christian story thus take their place within the developing whole. The unity of the divine and the human is a necessary part of the process, but in order for this divine-human unity to be grasped as a certainty it has actually to happen as something seen and experienced in the flesh. There is a sense, therefore, in which revelation in Christ tells us something we might already have known, because the truths expressed in it are universal and accessible to reason. Hence there need be no conflict between the particular historical claims of the Christian faith and a comprehensive (i.e. Hegelian) philosophy. The particular claims are important only because they give us a fixed emblematic reference point.

In a word, Hegel sought to rescue Christian faith from the contingencies of history. He showed us our place in the world as rational beings bound together in a truly free community, destined to know itself through the disclosure of the universal mind, which is the mind of God. There was a grandeur about his vision which can meet some of the worries about disproportion. Even the idea that the events of the incarnation are in some way representational, rather than necessarily unique and decisive, has its counterpart in ordinary Christian belief that there is an incarnational or sacramental principle to be discerned in the world, and that human nature itself bears marks of the union between the human and the divine. A universalised Christ belongs within universal history and, by implication, within the universe itself.

But Kierkegaard would have none of it. With superb irony he demonstrated the absurdity of supposing that all Christ did was somehow to reveal to us what is universally true, and what can in principle be known by other means. Christ is not an idea, but one who meets us. The unique significance of the incarnation lies in the fact that God meets us in a form which allows us to reject him. To know God is not to discern the highest product of our own thought, but to have a decisive encounter with one who transcends the possibilities of reason, yet loves us and invites us to respond to him in the paradox of his obscurity. The key, therefore, is faith, faith that it is the seemingly absurd, simple and provincial events of Christ's life, death and resurrection, which bring us into contact with a reality no amount of thought can reach. And it is precisely because they are not general ideas, but events located in a particular place and time, that anybody in any place or at any time can have equal access to them. Kierkegaard, in other words, gloried in the very things which made Feynman turn aside. He also put his finger on what it is about Hegel's philosophy that to many Christians made it seem so repellent.

If being a Christian is more like falling in love than solving a philosophical problem, then the concreteness of its central claims, its focus on an individual life, are the very characteristics which make this possible. Kierkegaard's famous parable about the dilemma of a noble king who loved a humble maiden, is a profound and moving exploration of the only kind of love which can unite the finite and the infinite, the temporal and the eternal, without corrupting either of them. For the king to bestow favours on the maiden, to raise her up to himself, would force her to remember what he wished only to forget, that he was a king and she had been just a humble maiden. The only way for love to express itself is by descending, by taking the form of a servant. 'Behold where he stands – the God! Where? There; do you not see him? He is God; and yet he has not a resting-place for his head, and he dares not lean on any man lest he cause him to be offended. He is God; and yet he picks his steps more carefully than if angels guided them, not to prevent his foot stumbling against a stone, but lest he trample human beings in the dust.'*

---

* Søren Kierkegaard, *Philosophical Fragments* (1844), especially Chapter 2. The whole book is an extended essay on the paradox of eternal truth as dependent on contingent historical events. Karl Barth's work is built on this paradox, inasmuch as his theology aims to be derived wholly from the particular events of the life, death and resurrection of Jesus Christ. The problem of evil, for example, is not treated as if it were some general philosophical conundrum, but is discussed in and through the particular story of Judas Iscariot. See *Church Dogmatics*, vol. 2:2, pp. 458–506. Donald Mackinnon explores this theme in his essay 'Philosophy and Christology' in *Borderlands of Theology* (Lutterworth, 1968), and Fergus Kerr has an excellent chapter on Barth's particularism in *Immortal Longings: Versions of Transcending Humanity* (SPCK, 1997).

27

Like Hegel, Kierkegaard too can repel thoughtful believers and unbelievers. In his case the demand that we face the absurd, that we accept faith as a leap into the dark, that we live by paradox, seems too far-fetched, too remote from even a modest rationality. Yet maybe this interpretation is unfair to him. Rationality may have to die but, as Kierkegaard's own powers of argument abundantly demonstrate, it rises again in another form. What is gained in the process is a realisation that questions about ultimate values cannot be answered by reason alone, but need inwardness, commitment and personal devotion.

I have given a brief sketch of this much-explored divide between Hegel and Kierkegaard because they helpfully set the limits within which some Christian response to the issues raised by Feynman has to be found. I have emphasised religious symbolism as one of the factors which pinpoint the necessity for tradition, and which require faith to be rooted within a particular historical context. To universalise this symbolism on the one hand, or on the other hand to locate it entirely in a unique personal encounter, effectively detaches it from its history. But there truly is a universal dimension to the themes on which Christian faith draws. I have already mentioned what I have called 'foundational experiences', and suggested that there may be some providential directions written into the nature of things. Maybe the meaning of such hints and signs can be discerned only with hindsight, when there are particular historical reasons for doing so. But those historical reasons need to be of kinds which are not so paradoxical, so remote from ordinary experience, that it is impossible to argue about them or to assess the value of the testimony on which they rest.

In short, we need both the universal and the particular, the grand vision and the human encounter. If my previous analogy with evolutionary theory is valid, a world shaped by contingent events does not have to be a world without overall purpose or meaning. When Dante wrote about 'The love that moves the sun and the other stars', he was expressing faith in a providential consistency and order. In the next chapter I shall be looking again

28

at this kind of faith and its difficulties. But Christians cannot avoid making some such universal claims. We also have to accept that we are limited to our human perspective, and it is hard to know what love was doing during the millions of years when the dinosaurs ruled the earth, or the thousands of millions of years before that. Perhaps love was simply letting the universe be, allowing it to evolve into whatever the freedom given to it enabled it to bring forth. The fact that at this point in time it has produced us may not be the end of the story. But we, unique among all the creatures that we know of, have the capacity to tell the story so far. Nor need there be any contradiction in interpreting it as the work of a noble king, a Kierkegaardian king, who hides himself in love so that we too are allowed to be whatever our exercise of freedom brings forth, and at whatever cost to the one who loves us. It is not a matter of necessity. The fact is that we can only tell this kind of story because it has actually been lived, and its very particularity, far from being a cause of offence, can be seen as a supreme affirmation of individual human worth within a universal process.*

Nevertheless there is a fragility about our knowing, which is inherent in the character of love. Love is a perpetual surprise, an impossible possibility. Its worst enemy is complacency, and that is why a complacent church can seem so deeply unattractive to those, like Feynman, who are aware of what life can offer in other ways, and who miss the authentic note of surprise and excitement. There are others for whom living with risk may be equally unattractive.[13]

---

* Kerr, op. cit. p. 163, where he is expounding Urs von Balthasar. The 'desacralization of nature . . . affords new opportunities for Christian faith. Finding ourselves alone in this demythologized universe, we discover that we human beings are the only sources of ultimate value. When we regard another human being as of such unique and intrinsic worth, we begin to suspect that this becomes visible only in the illuminating perspective of the Christian tradition. The collapse of religion clears the way for the appearance of Christianity in all its specificity. Indeed, previously, the biblical world itself was "almost like an episode, clarifying the deep embrace of infinite and finite freedom", seldom or never allowed to stand out in its historical particularity.'

I believe that Christians have to accept the vulnerability of a faith which bases its universal claims on events which are subject to historical scrutiny. The one is as essential as the other, both a coming to terms with the immensities of space and time, and an acknowledgement that they can only be given a Christian interpretation through a faith which is rooted in the contingencies of history, and so can give meaning to individual lives. In fact it belongs to the very heart of Christianity that the infinite is made present to us in a finite life, and the eternal made present in time. It is in one sense shocking that so much of ultimate import should depend on events which might have been otherwise. But perhaps we might see this also as characteristic of the surprisingness of love, which does not have to have precise plans in order to give eternal significance to contingent happenings.

Within Christianity the continuity of tradition and the accumulation of significance in traditional symbolism, create a kind of historical stability. In so far as this occurs in a community which is open to criticism and constantly ready to have conversation within itself and with those outside it, we probably have the best model for accepting historical vulnerability without being paralysed by it.

Those whom I have called healthy-minded unbelievers might wish for something more. But if it really is love which moves the sun and the other stars, then for us human beings the evidence for it is more likely to be embodied in a human life and a human death, than set out in a clever argument.

3

Explanation and Understanding

Unbelief, like belief, has its myths and symbols which do not relate as securely as they might to the happenings on which they are supposed to be based. This is certainly true of the two most notorious encounters, frequently cited as paradigms of the conflict between open-minded science on the one hand and obscurantist Christian theology on the other. In the popular mythology of unbelief, Galileo and Darwin have taken their place as the scientific heroes who changed our perceptions of the world, in the face of prestigious but ultimately futile religious opposition. Their victories paved the way for a new class of rational unbelievers, who were able thus to rid themselves of superstitious adherence to outmoded authorities. It is a powerful myth, but in neither case does it bear much resemblance to what historians have been able to discover, or to what was actually at stake.[1]

Galileo's dispute with Cardinal Bellarmine over the Copernican interpretation of the solar system was not primarily about the authority of Scripture, or of the Church, or even of the Aristotelian world-view. These were side issues in a much more fundamental philosophical conflict which still has relevance to the role of science in human understanding. The encounter took place at a time when the notion of what it is to be scientific was in process of being formed.[2] At the heart of Galileo's achievement was his use of numerical concepts, abstracted from ordinary experience, as a counter-intuitive basis for explaining otherwise familiar phenomena. He was the first person, for example, to treat time as an abstract quantifiable parameter of physical events.[3] He conceived time as a dimension, rather than as something one simply experiences, and his success in analysing motion depended entirely on this unprecedented feat of imagination. He saw beyond the experiential world of falling bodies to another level of reality in which, as he said, 'the book of nature is written in mathematical characters.'

Translate this into Copernican astronomy, and one comes to the heart of the conflict with the Church. Was the Copernican system a mathematically convenient, albeit counter-intuitive, way of describing the movement of the heavens, or was it more than that, a description of what was really the case, a straightforward reading of the book of nature? Galileo's claim to be describing reality was reinforced by his observations of Jupiter's satellites, themselves a miniature Copernican system. The symbol of bigoted churchmen refusing to look at them has ever since been a focus for scientific scorn.

However, the arguments were not all on one side. The Jesuits, of whom Bellarmine was one, were themselves competent astronomers with an empirical approach, but they were also deeply conscious of the limitations of unaided reason in trying to pass beyond mere appearances to a description of reality. It has been suggested that questions about appearance and reality were particularly acute for Roman Catholic theologians in the immediate post-reformation period, in view of their relevance to the doctrine of transubstantiation.[4] Whatever the truth of that, the philosophical question is with us still, expressed in classic form by Kant. Can we ever reach beyond phenomena to ultimate reality? Or are we for ever stuck with the way things appear to us, limited by our human mode of perception? The same questions arise in the philosophy of science, in the never-ending dispute between realism and instrumentalism. Although most scientists ignore the difficulties and behave as if they were realists, there are fundamental areas of science, especially in quantum theory, where the issue is unavoidable. If, as is claimed, the form of quantum phenomena depends on the way they are investigated, then appearances are the most we can ever hope for.[5]

32

This is not to say that Cardinal Bellarmine and the pope were right all along. On Copernicus they were clearly wrong. Many scientific theories are demonstrably more than just a convenient way of ordering empirical results. As observable phenomena the planets really do go round the sun. It has become increasingly clear that atoms and molecules are not just useful theoretical entities, but are in some circumstances almost as directly observable, and hence as 'real' as tables and chairs. Yet at another level of understanding, scientific knowledge, like all knowledge, is a mental construct, a particular way of ordering experience, the reading of a mathematical book. It is also dependent on a belief system which encompasses such indefinable concepts as causality, coherence and rationality itself. The popular symbolism of open enquiry versus obdurate authoritarianism hides much more complex and, in some respects still unresolved, issues.

The British Association meeting of 1860 at which T. H. Huxley defended Darwinism against the Bishop of Oxford has attained the same mythical status as the story of Galileo, though precise details of what was said on that occasion are notoriously unclear.* This encounter, like its predecessor, is usually interpreted as a straight conflict between scientific discovery and outmoded appeals to authority and prejudice. There was undoubtedly something of

---

* The story has been told many times, e.g. in Adrian Desmond and James Moore's *Darwin* (Michael Joseph, 1991), pp. 492–99. The most careful historical analysis is probably to be found in J. R. Lucas, 'Wilberforce and Huxley: A Legendary Encounter', *The Historical Journal*, vol. 22: 2 (1979), pp. 313–30. Lucas makes a convincing case for believing that Wilberforce uttered no personal remarks about Huxley at all, and that what he actually said was 'If anyone one were to be willing to trace his descent through an ape as his *grandfather*, would he be willing to trace his descent similarly on the side of his *grandmother*.' It was an unworthy remark, appealing to a kind of inverse feminism, but it was not personal, and it seems to have been doctored subsequently to provide an occasion for Huxley's famous put-down, which was not actually recorded at the time. The real point at issue was not so much a clash between science and religion, but what would now be called a paradigm shift, a new way of interpreting the whole of biology, which inevitably aroused deep-seated controversy on the basis of what was then insufficient evidence.

the latter element in the case made by the bishop, just as on the other side scientific impartiality was not immune from seething resentment at the clerical monopoly in the universities. The bishop was unwise as he tried to lighten the atmosphere, in what had hitherto been an abysmally dull meeting, by making jokes on a matter which could rouse high passions. The only thing anybody now remembers about the meeting is a facetious remark about Huxley's supposed apeish grandparents, the sense of which has almost certainly been distorted in the telling. But what the myth does not convey is that here too there were serious scientific arguments on both sides. The scientific community at the time was itself divided, and there was a gaping hole at the centre of Darwinian theory, which was not filled until the rediscovery of Mendel's theory of inheritance 40 years later in 1900. Despite being able to make well-supported scientific criticisms of Darwin's thesis, the bishop chose to bolster his arguments with a misguided appeal to quasi-scientific evidence in the Bible, which was bound to weaken his case rather than strengthen it. This does not mean, however, that those who initially opposed Darwin were mere obscurantists. The idea that natural selection could do all that was proposed for it was strongly counter-intuitive and hotly contested by prominent experts in the field. There was also a serious theoretical issue about how far an unrepeatable historical process could be scientifically proven. It is hardly surprising that most, but by no means all, religious believers chose the side which supported their previous convictions.

I begin with these two symbolic moments in a long history, because they have come to represent what was happening constantly in less dramatic ways as scientific discoveries seemed to make progressive inroads into Christian belief. At no point was the story as simple as the mythology might seem to suggest. There was, however, a dangerous assumption at the root of much Christian apologetic, which left it vulnerable to this kind of erosion. It was the assumption that science, or natural philosophy as it was then, must somehow prove, or provide support for, or at least leave sufficient space for, claims to religious truth. Those

34

who shared this assumption ignored the fact that science is omnivorous; on its own ground it has no resting point until it has accounted for everything and explained it.

The danger in trying to validate theology by appealing to natural philosophy is all too apparent in the story of Samuel Clarke. He was a brilliant young contemporary of Sir Isaac Newton, and acted as his theological interpreter and apologist.[6] Newton, like Galileo, had to work with a distinction between the apparent and the real. Real motion, for instance, was motion within the absolute framework of space, as contrasted with the relative motions between different bodies, which are all that can actually be observed. Newton believed he could deduce the existence of the absolute framework, just as he could deduce the existence of force as the means through which matter made its presence felt. Thus the reality behind the wonders observed in the heavens was disclosed as an amazing mechanical contrivance, and the fact that it worked within an absolute framework, unchangeable and eternal, was immediately seen to have theological implications. How do these qualities of unchangeableness and eternity, it was asked, relate to the attributes of God?

It was Clarke's role to fashion these scientific insights into a convincing theology, which he did with such success that for a time he was rated as second only to John Locke in the ranks of English philosophers. In essence his line of argument followed the familiar cosmological and teleological proofs of the existence of God, but its starting point was the cosmos as disclosed by Newton, the eternal framework, the orderliness now fully discerned in nature, together with the observed element of contingency in the distribution of matter. From these Clarke deduced the necessary existence of an independent, immutable and intelligent being, all-powerful and infinitely wise, and imbued with liberty and choice. I am not concerned here with the details of the argument. The point is that it was founded on the Newtonian conception of the cosmos, and thus rested ultimately on science. Clarke was trying to meet the atheists of his day on their own ground by basing philosophy, theology and morality on a grand theory of mechanics.

Forty years after his death his whole argument was turned on its head in the first modern systematic treatise on materialism, Baron d'Holbach's *The System of Nature*. It was the most powerful atheistic tract of the Enlightenment which, section by section, took to pieces Clarke's argument by grounding each of his propositions about ultimate reality in nature rather than in God. Newton was right to start with the phenomena of the natural world, and to see matter in motion as constituting all its parts. But, went the argument, there is no need to postulate anything beyond matter in motion, because every phenomenon can, at least in principle, be explained in terms of it. We know nature as a system because it is intelligible, but whether we impose that intelligibility or discover it, is unanswerable because there is no way of moving from the apparent to the real. It is enough to know that matter is eternal, immutable and self-existent, precisely the attributes ascribed by Clarke to God, and thereby to rid ourselves of the contradictions and illogicalities of theology. Impenetrable mysteries about ultimate reality are best left on one side.

Such an account omits, of course, a great deal which may need to be said about such difficult problems as human consciousness, the relation between the observer and what is observed, and the basis of human rationality, but these were not part of Clarke's or Newton's arguments either. The clear lesson to be drawn is that a theological argument which starts with nature is likely also to end with nature. Such a theology, in other words, digs its own grave by generating its own atheism. Michael Buckley, who has told this story in detail, puts it thus:

> 'Atheism is the secret of that religious reflection which justifies the sacred and its access to the sacred primarily through its own transmogrification into another form of human knowledge or practice . . . as though religion had to become philosophy to remain religion. The unique character of religious knowledge does not survive this reduction. Another discipline cannot be made more fundamental and religion its corollary or epiphenomenon. Religion, with all of its

intersubjectivities, cannot but be destroyed if dissolved into some other human experience in order to justify its most critical cognitive claims. Eventually such a dissolution will out as atheism.'[7]*

It is a warning which extends beyond the controversies of the Enlightenment. Darwin did for the argument from design what Holbach's materialistic philosophy had tried to do in a much cruder fashion, by depending on the inherent creativeness of nature to account for its richness and diversity. I referred in the first chapter to the Victorian love of 'divine contrivances', evidences of God's handiwork in the minutiae of biology. It is still possible to observe such 'contrivances' in awe and wonder, and to use them as occasions for praise. But the argument from contrivances to a designer God implies that God is in some direct way part of the explanation of why they are what they are. The assumption that this is what post-Darwinian theologians are actually saying is still to be found in almost all the polemical literature which uses evolution as a stick with which to beat religion.[8] God as a potential explanation is compared with evolution as a potential explanation, and found to be wanting. What, asks the critic, does the notion of God as designer add to what the biologist can already tell us? If in a few instances the biologist is uncertain what to say, experience suggests that the theologian who exploits lack of scientific knowledge is bound to be refuted sooner or later. Because many apologists continue to fall into this trap, atheism is still being generated by inadequate theologies which rely too heavily on other disciplines for their justification.

On what then should belief be based? I referred earlier to a neglect of consciousness in Holbach's *System of Nature*. There were theologians ready to fill this gap, of whom Schleiermacher is

---

* Brooke and Cantor, op. cit. pp. 150–52, take a less negative view of natural theology than Buckley. For instance it is sometimes necessary for religious apologists to use scientific arguments to counter criticisms that a particular scientific theory destroys the credibility of belief. But this is not the same as trying to base religious belief on science.

the obvious example. The revolution whereby theology turned inwards, to feelings, to self-consciousness, to self-analysis, may have helped to rescue religion from the embrace of atheistic materialism, but in the end it too generated an atheism of its own. This was partly, as we shall see in the next chapter, by reaction against the kind of dependence on God which seemed to deny human freedom and adulthood. We have heard much in the twentieth century about humanity come of age. More generally the turn inwards to the self had the paradoxical effect of making God in some sense dependent on human experience, from which it was but a short step to treating God as a mere projection of human needs.[9]

This propensity of belief to breed its own form of unbelief creates a dilemma for Christians. If there are dangers in turning to philosophy, or science, or the world of nature, or our own inner world, to help ground our Christian belief, where do we turn? The traditional Christian answer is that we turn to Jesus Christ, despite the hazards of relying on a fragile historical record. Pascal, as usual, saw the point:

> 'All who seek God without Jesus Christ, and who rest in nature, either find no light to satisfy them, or come to form for themselves a means of knowing God and serving him without a mediator. Thereby they fall either into atheism, or into deism, two things which the Christian religion abhors almost equally.'[10]

This is not just the simple appeal to revelation that it might appear to be. In Pascal, as in classic Christian philosophy, there was a subtle relationship between what reason could discern about the necessary conditions for its existence, and what needed somehow to be given in history, in personal experience and in the experience of the Christian community. The standard philo-sophical arguments for the existence of God depended on reasoning about such abstractions as causality, contingency, neces-sary being and intelligible order, but their conclusion was not a theological construction. It was an act of recognition – 'this all men speak of as God'. In a similar way, the awesome wonders of the universe and the mystery of personal awareness can still lead the thinking mind to recognise God, even if only as 'the transcendent'.★ The mistake is to regard this as sufficient, to abstract it from the context of real lived religion, and so to end up with a philosophical concept which might just as well be reinterpreted atheistically, or at best impersonally.

Pascal managed to retain the right balance, to look at the evidences of nature, but also to acknowledge their ambivalence and their need for illumination from some other source. 'If the world existed to instruct man of God, his divinity would shine through every part of it in an indisputable manner . . . All appearance indicates neither a total exclusion nor a manifest presence of divinity, but the presence of a God who hides himself.'[11] The reason for this was identified by Pascal as the ambivalence of human beings themselves who are 'neither angels nor brutes', wretched in their unworthiness of God, and great because they are conscious of what they are missing. God is partly hidden and partly revealed 'since it is equally dangerous for man to know God without knowing his own wretchedness, and to know his own wretchedness without knowing God.'[12]

If it is true that God is both present to us and hidden in the natural world, we can begin to see why attempts to deduce his existence, or use him as an explanation, end in failure. The hints

---

★ Fergus Kerr, *Immortal Longings: Versions of Transcending Humanity* (SPCK, 1997). The book identifies unacknowledged theological preconceptions in a number of modern philosophers. Wittgenstein, for instance, was much concerned with religious belief in his later writings, as in this thought from *Culture and Value* (1994) p. 97e. 'Life can educate you to "believing in God". And *experiences* too are what do this but not visions or other sense experiences, which show "the existence of this being", but e.g sufferings of various sorts. And they do not show us God as a sense experience does an object, nor do they give rise to *conjectures* about him. Experiences, thoughts – life can force the concept on us. So perhaps it is similar to the concept "object".' He is not, of course, saying that God is an object, but that the concept of God can be as necessary for the interpretation of some aspects of our experience as is the concept 'object' for the interpretation of other aspects.

are there, the desire to make theological sense of the whole range of human experience, but without the starting point of an encounter already embedded in the history of faith, all that is likely to be discovered is a reflection of our own concerns. This is not a conclusion, however, which is likely to mollify the rationalistic unbeliever, since it is precisely this appeal to a starting point outside rational argument which will be rejected as mere fideism, an escape route from reason into faith. The believer would want to ask in reply whether reason can ever operate in a context wholly devoid of previously interpreted experience. The stories of Galileo and Darwin illustrate how what were once presented as straightforward conflicts, can be understood differently against the background of more thorough social, historical and philosophical analysis. It is this attempt to set scientific explanation in a larger frame of understanding, that may offer a way of avoiding confrontations arising out of the failure to take account of different aims, assumptions and types of evidence.

A formal distinction between explanation and understanding was introduced towards the end of the last century by the German philosopher Wilhelm Dilthey.[13] Much water has flowed under the bridge since then, but it is worth returning for a moment to the source, because one of the peculiarities of the English-speaking world is that it failed to adopt Dilthey's further distinction between the natural sciences and the human sciences. English speakers have thus become used to working with a stark contrast between a monolithic concept of 'science', and all other forms of so-called knowledge which are 'non-scientific', and hence deemed to be inferior.

According to Dilthey explanation is the goal of the natural sciences, and understanding the goal of the human sciences. By the latter he meant all that concerns the living wholeness of human beings, including their social, historical, religious and aesthetic context. To understand is to be able to describe and interpret this total culture, and to express its meaning for those involved in it. To explain, on the other hand, is to relate precisely identifiable and analysable aspects of experience to one another.

40

The distinction is not clear-cut. Understanding in this broad sense may well have to include explanation. Insights, say, from psychology or physiology may be needed to explain someone's behaviour, before this can be interpreted within the broader context of their own self-understanding and behavioural goals. At the same time there is a major difference between explaining a person's movements in terms of brain activity, nerve impulses and muscular contractions, and understanding them as actions intended for some purpose. The contexts, the aims, the tools and the language of inquiry are different in the two cases, yet both can be rational activities, subject to criticism and open to correction. In this sense they are both sciences – at least in Germany.

Dilthey's concept of 'understanding' also had reference to understanding the past, and was thus an important component of the then growing debate about hermeneutics. In fact the so-called hermeneutic circle, the interplay between our own pre-judgements and the texts or evidences we are seeking to interpret, defines admirably the kind of to-ing and fro-ing between evidence and interpretation which critical understanding requires.[14] What can be seen as happening in a relatively rigorous manner when scholars try to interpret texts, can in theory also happen in the process of living, as unconscious assumptions and conscious beliefs are brought to bear on actual experience and, as a result, either refined, abandoned or reinforced. In real life, of course, things are never quite as simple as this. Particular beliefs may change, as when a historian may have to revise an opinion about the religious significance of Galileo's trial. But deep-seated beliefs, such as those about the way the world is, or the values we should live by, tend to be much more resistant to change, especially when they form part of a community consciousness. Similar resistance occurs when fundamental concepts or modes of explanation within the natural sciences are threatened. In fact it is obvious that in both the natural and the human sciences the majority of people are unwilling to dispose of a tradition of practical wisdom, until there is something manifestly better to put in its place. There is also an evolutionary argument in favour of a certain conservatism of belief, in that the passage of time must tend to adapt beliefs more closely to reality, just as it has adapted bodies to live in this world and not another. But one also has to admit that some organisms, like some people, find an environmental niche which suits them, snuggle down there and let change pass them by.

My reason for digressing into this somewhat dated, and much fought over, territory is to make the point that 'understanding', in Dilthey's sense – the attempt to interpret lived experience in its total context – can be a rational activity, despite the fact that there are many instances when it is not. The human sciences, including theology, struggle to define concepts as precise and clear as those used in the natural sciences, but they invariably fail for the simple reason that most of the factors in human life which matter to human beings are inherently resistant to this kind of treatment. To suppose otherwise is to falsify them.

Furthermore the relationship between what is being studied and those who are doing the studying differs between the natural and the human sciences. The study of the experience of being human requires a kind of empathy which is inappropriate in the scientific study of the non-human world. Sciences, such as sociology and anthropology, which straddle the human and the non-human worlds, tend to be beset by controversies about how far those studying them should be personally involved in the communities they are observing – a point to which I shall be returning in Chapter 5.[15]

There is also the challenge, particularly strong nowadays in the human sciences, of all that goes under the name of deconstruction. No doubt it has its uses, but simply to abandon belief that there can be rational and constructive processes of criticism, leading to insights of permanent value, in such fields as history, theology, literature, poetry and music, seems to me a betrayal of civilisation. If there is really felt to be no difference in value between a Beethoven symphony and the latest pop song, it is difficult to see why anything at all should be valued, other than as a means of immediate gratification. The testing by time, to which I have already referred, may be more complex and uncertain in the

42

human sciences than in the natural sciences, but the fact that it is possible to identify enduring themes, values and achievements running through most civilisations is evidence that there are genuine truths to be discerned about the human world.[16] There can be a directness, too, in the understanding of life as it is actually lived, which need not be undermined by the attempts of the natural sciences to explain it in terms of other supposedly more 'real' factors, whether genes, or hormones, or computer models of the brain, or hitherto unperceived social forces.

It is within this mode of understanding that belief can best stake its claim against the rational sceptic. I have been arguing that a rational religious faith should not be in the business of offering alternative scientific explanations. Philosophically orientated religious insights may nevertheless have a role within the natural sciences in criticising unwarranted claims, and examining the assumptions, such as the uniformity of nature, on which scientific rationality has traditionally been based. A recent rather wild suggestion that some phenomena might be more explicable if the laws of physics had gradually changed over time, has highlighted this particular assumption as one which cannot simply be taken for granted. Likewise the belief that the universe is comprehensible, and that certain ways of thinking which we call rational are appropriate for disclosing this comprehensibility, are not plucked out of the air, but form part of a long intellectual tradition with a history of its own. The fact that there are other intellectual traditions, and that typical Western thinking is now being radically criticised from within, need not lead to the conclusion that all claims to knowledge, even scientific knowledge, are relative. But it does point to the need to justify the tradition, to stress its practical communal character, its dependence on open dialogue, interpretation, evaluation and the hammering out of agreements about relevant criteria – all of them activities that are themselves part of the wider context of learning from our total experience, which Dilthey called 'understanding'.

None of what I have said so far need relate directly to religious faith, except in the sense that rational faith itself has to go through this same process of historical testing within an argumentative community, as it tries to respond to new knowledge in the light of its foundation experiences. To understand the world as God's creation, for instance, does not entail putting forward an alternative theological-scientific explanation of how it came to be. It is to draw scientific insights into a parallel tradition of thinking, in which questions of meaning, value and appropriate response are central. It is to wonder at the sheer surprising existence of things, and to interpret them as gifts of love and as a potential for blessing. It is about the lived experience of responding to the real beyond all appearances, in the light of those fragile moments in history when encounter with the real has been life-changing. At a more philosophical level it is about an awareness of contingency, a might-not-have-been-ness, a sense of gratuitousness, which can be enormously heightened by reflection on the circumstances of our own coming into being. The odds are staggering against each of us having the precise genetic make-up which constitutes our individuality. To experience life in these terms, and to know ourselves as addressed by a transcendent reality, and to interpret that reality in terms of self-giving love, is a particularly Christian way of understanding the larger context within which cosmological explanations also have their place.

There may well be differences of perception and proportion, as I suggested in the previous chapter. For instance, there is a place for rational argument about whether the cosmos as described by the natural sciences must necessarily be the way it is, if lives capable of understanding it are to be possible. The so-called anthropic principle highlights the connection between the existence of life in at least one part of the universe, and the extraordinary fine-tuning of the physical constants that determine the way matter behaves. A very small change in any one of these would have resulted in a universe in which the complex molecules necessary for life in any imaginable form could not have evolved. The principle has been much exploited by some theologians.[17] But if we take the story of past mistakes seriously, the principle is not to be interpreted as a proof from physics of God's existence. At most it is a helpful sign that scientific explanation and religious understanding have areas of overlap, in which there are good grounds for thinking that creatures like us were meant to be.

There are many other contexts in which one can try to relate scientific explanation to some larger process of understanding, but I end with one which raises questions about the scientific enterprise itself. What are the natural sciences for? Justifications range from satisfying curiosity, and enlarging knowledge for its own sake, to helping us survive in a competitive world, and improving the quality of human life.[18] The type of justification makes a difference, because it sets the agenda for what is actually done. At one end of the scale is an ideal of knowledge which is value-free, objective and impersonal, and thus held to be universally valid by virtue of this detachment from personal bias and self-interest. It is what, I suspect, many scientists would like to think of themselves as doing, with the ultimate goal of explanation being found at the rarified extremes of the so-called hard sciences – the final cosmological equation which wraps it all up. For the vast majority, however, the reality is quite different, not only in terms of the reasons why they are employed, but also because of the assumptions within which they have to work. Even in theory science has never been value-free, but has depended at its most basic level on value judgements about what is or is not science. Science aimed at human good must necessarily include a huge raft of other value judgements about what makes for human flourishing. Most scientific theory simply takes for granted much of the common-sense world of ordinary human understanding, in which we do not seriously doubt the validity of such notions as truth, honesty and rationality. This is not to suggest that arbitrary considerations of value should enter into the process of justifying scientific results, though some considerations about what matters, and what does not, will undoubtedly be present. As enterprises, however, the natural sciences cannot dispense with pre-judgements, enthusiasm, commitment, a vision of worthwhile ends and community loyalty, in fact just those qualities which are regarded with such suspicion when found within communities of faith.

Galileo and Darwin both brought about profound changes in human understanding, and over the years those changes of perception have been incorporated into religious belief systems without destroying them. Controversy is probably inevitable as such incorporation takes place; in fact, as I have repeatedly said, it is through controversy that mistakes and misunderstandings are eventually weeded out, and understanding grows. It is a process which has often been presented as a struggle between belief and unbelief, with unbelief progressively occupying the territory ceded to science. I have been advocating an alternative way of describing it – as the means by which rational traditions of thought have always developed. Beliefs which attach themselves too closely to particular scientific explanations eventually generate unbelief. But a faith which draws on its historical foundations to interpret life as actually experienced, and which can use such interpretation to expose narrowness of understanding in the present, and which finds within itself many of the same fundamental values on which the tradition of scientific thought depends, may still remain vulnerable to historical investigation, but need have no quarrel with the natural sciences. The Christian faith has shown itself remarkably adept at incorporating new knowledge. What we understand is what our history has made it possible for us to understand.[19] This is why a profound and life-giving tradition, which for two thousand years has provided access to hopes and possibilities and powers which transcend us, should neither be too disturbed by, nor hitched too prematurely to, the latest scientific star.

4

Moral Autonomy

There is a famous little incident in Dostoevsky's novel *The Devils* in which one of the characters describes a drinking party with a group of infantry officers. 'They were discussing atheism and I need hardly say they made short work of God. They were squealing with delight. By the way, Shatov declares that if there's to be a rising in Russia we must begin with atheism. Maybe it's true. One grizzled old stager of a captain sat mum, not saying a word. All at once he stands up in the middle of the room and says aloud as though speaking to himself: "If there's no God, how can I be a captain then?" ' The friend to whom the story was told, commented: 'He expressed a rather sensible idea.'[1]

It is a theme to which Dostoevsky returns again and again. Remove God as the lynchpin of morality and social order, and everything collapses. How can there be a hierarchy when there is no sense of that which stands above us and has power over us? How can there be morality without some ideal which is not simply of our own choosing? In his novels we find character after character exploring what it is to live without morality and order, in the name of freedom, rebellion, self-discovery or disillusionment. 'O freedom, what liberties are taken in your name!' as a wit once put it. Dostoevsky agonised about belief in God in a world so manifestly disordered and cruel. He feared that if the story of the God-man could no longer be believed, man himself must become God, and when man is God, everything is permitted. He saw himself as standing on the edge of an abyss, the same abyss over which Nietzsche was later to plunge.

My aim in this chapter is to illustrate what William James might have called twice-born unbelief – the rejection of religious belief not, as in the previous two chapters, with polite indifference or academic disrespect, but with passionate moral intensity. Both Dostoevsky and Nietzsche were setting out in their different ways the consequences of conversion to unbelief, of a revolt against Christianity and a denial of its fundamental ideals of goodness. Dostoevsky struggled with faith all his life, and held on to it in typical Russian Orthodox style through a passive acceptance of suffering. He said of his own writings, 'Even in Europe there have never been atheistic expressions of such power. Consequently, I do not believe in Christ and his confession as a child, but my hosanna has come through a great *furnace of doubt*.'[2]

Nietzsche, a son of the manse, would have none of this. His was a deliberate war on Christianity, condemned for precisely this exaltation of weakness and suffering, and for what he called its 'slave morality'. 'The inoffensiveness of the weak, his cowardice, his uneluctable standing and waiting at doors, are being given honorific titles such as "patience"; to be *unable* to avenge oneself is called to be *unwilling* to avenge oneself – even forgiveness (for they know not what *they* do – we alone know what *they* do) . . . I'm sure they are quite miserable, all these whisperers and small-time counterfeiters, even though they huddle close together for warmth. But they tell me that this very misery is a sign of their election by God, that one beats the dog one loves best'[3] and so on through pages and pages of pointed satire. There is the unforgettable passage in Zarathustra where Nietzsche describes the essentially unheroic nature of these weaklings whom he calls *Last Man*: 'a man must have chaos yet within him to be able to give birth to a dancing star . . . Alas! the day cometh when man shall give birth to no more stars . . . Behold! I show you the Last Man. What is love? What is creation? What is desire? What is a star? asketh the Last Man, and he blinketh! Then earth will have grown small, and upon it shall hop the Last Man which maketh all things small. His kind is inexterminable like the ground-flea; the Last Man liveth longest. "We have discovered happiness," say the Last Men, and they blink.'[4] Contrast that picture with the heart of Zarathustra's message: 'Man is a thing to be surmounted.'[5] He is a bridge, not an end. His aim should be to exercise his will, not to renounce it, to find virtue, not in unselfishness but in the courage to be a self. This is what Nietzsche understands by autonomy. The autonomous man has 'developed his own, independent, long-range will, which dares to make promises; he has a proud and vigorous consciousness of what he has achieved, a sense of power and freedom, of absolute accomplishment. This fully emancipated man, master of his will, who dares to make promises – how should he not be aware of his superiority over those who are unable to stand security for themselves?'[6]

Nietzsche is so quotable that it is tempting to continue. My concern, however, is not with Nietzsche himself but to illustrate how present-day ideas about moral autonomy were nurtured in the rich soil of nineteenth-century rebellion against God. There was often a strength and nobility in this rebellion, which needs to be treated with the utmost seriousness. It had begun to take shape in the Enlightenment, but the seeds were planted long before. There is a revealing precursor in the grudging respect paid to Milton's Satan in *Paradise Lost*. The hints of nobility in Satan's determination to persist at all costs – 'Better to reign in Hell than serve in Heaven'★ – the disturbing arbitrariness of God's demand for obedience, and the way in which the whole set-up is presented as having been rigged to put this obedience to the test,† strongly

---

★ See, for example, Book I, lines 252ff:

> '. . . rather seek
> Our own good from ourselves, and from our own
> Live to ourselves, though in this vast recess,
> Free and to none accountable, preferring
> Hard liberty before the easy yoke
> Of servile pomp . . .'

† Book III struggles to make sense of a predestined fall, for which humanity nevertheless remains responsible. But the first lines of the whole poem set the tone for the rest of it:

suggest that something had gone badly wrong with the underlying concept of God.

If disobedience really was the primal sin, and if God's intention in creating humanity was to keep us in subservience and to establish our dependence on him, then it would seem that the essential nature of God was conceived as power. Milton, of course, was not alone in depicting God in such terms. There is a strong strand of biblical teaching about the almightiness of God, which carries the suggestion that his power is just an infinitely larger and more dangerous version of human power, electric in its devastating effects on those struck by it. One of the consequences of such a concept of power is that what might have been a holy and loving fear of God in the contemplation of awesome mystery, can turn into resentful trepidation in the face of superior force, until in the long run subservience to power leads to its rejection. As Phillip Blond has recently put it: 'Once the nothingness of creatures has been figured as a lack of power formed in reference to a corresponding fearsome and utterly powerful whole, then we can already see the path to modernity's demand for human self-assertion.'[7] It is a further example of what I was describing in the last chapter – a distortion of theism giving rise to its own form of atheism.

It is not true, though, that moral revolt against God's power necessarily leads to the horrors foreseen by Dostoevsky. In fact in some instances quite the reverse. For some people the sense of autonomy, and the realisation that if good is to be done it has to be done by us, can liberate reserves of benevolence which might have been frozen by a fatalistic reliance on God. In the words of an American writer, 'the moment one loses confidence in God or immortality' one becomes 'more self-reliant, more courageous, and the more solicitous to aid where only human aid is possible.'[8]

The playwright David Hare has made a similar point about

'Of Man's first disobedience, and the fruit
Of that forbidden tree whose mortal taste
Brought death into the World, and all our woe . . .'

the liberation from religious sanctions and rewards. When doing research for his play, *Racing Demon*, he visited many clergy and commented afterwards on what he called 'the fatal tendency to have one eye on this life and one eye on a second . . . The best Christians are the ones who work as if there is no tomorrow. But I still could not help observing in the months spent with my vicars that there is a subtle loss of urgency, a certain psychological softness in the way you approach life if you subscribe to a religion which teaches you that there is something else beside life itself. There is a moment at which your mind drifts upwards. Justice on this earth seems to matter less to you if justice will one day be delivered in another.'[9] Like many others, he also has much to say about the extent to which religions can foster priggishness, spite, hypocrisy and violence. Today's world has no need of further reminders about the unhealthy intersection between nationalism and religious fanaticism.

Leave aside for the moment the question whether all this criticism of religion is deserved. I cite it as an example of morally serious unbelief which frequently, by its very unpretentiousness, manages to avoid some of the worst pitfalls of religiously based morality. There may be less happy consequences, though, of the refusal to countenance any kind of transcendent moral authority which might seem contrary to personal autonomy, even when the rejection is not as violent as that of Nietzsche and Dostoevsky's conspirators. Advocates of self-assertiveness and self-reliance can be so anxious to avoid any hint of external moral constraints, that they fall straight into the old mistake of supposing that it is possible to have freedom without law. The reality, demonstrated again and again in the political sphere by the experience of anarchy, is that freedom necessitates law, because law is the only basis on which freedom can be guaranteed and shared. The relationship between moral autonomy and public standards of morality is no less crucial.

Some of the practical dangers of forgetting this balance between internal aspirations and external constraints are already apparent in the current enthusiasm for human rights. Rights are attractive because they hold out the prospect of universal standards of justice without any potentially controversial reference to beliefs or obligations. Cut loose, however, from a generally accepted tradition of beliefs and obligations, they can result in an explosion of claims to personal rights of every imaginable kind, so that the whole concept quickly degenerates into a self-centred scramble for what each autonomous individual can demand from that universal provider – the state.[10]

Adherence to a moral standard, by contrast, entails setting individual needs and desires in a larger context of mutual responsibilities. At stake here is the difference between autonomy and authority, between grounding choices in something which lies inherently within the self, my rights, my freedom, my self-fulfilment, or responding to what Paul Ricoeur has described as 'the exteriority of the other who summons me to responsibility, [and] who constitutes me as a responsible subject'.[11]

In making this contrast I have no wish to belittle the importance of rights as such, particularly when they are identified as the rights of the individual against state oppression. In the context of such oppression an appeal to universal human rights can be a powerful instrument of justice, and the relative independence of rights from exclusive religious beliefs can be an advantage in a pluralist world. But their very success in this political field increases the temptation to multiply them in contexts well outside it. The assumption that every need, and in extreme cases every want, must somehow be dignified as a right, serves only to institutionalise a kind of selfishness. An appeal to rights, in preference to an exploration of moral obligations, may give a sense of urgency to types of fulfilment which are good and desirable in themselves, but the wider consequences of doing so tend to be overlooked. In the field of medicine, for example, it is already possible to observe how the valuable progress towards greater patient autonomy is becoming increasingly slanted by the language of rights in directions which raise huge, and largely unresolved, problems about the proper limits of medical interference. This is especially evident in the field of reproductive technology, the very title of which hints at the de-moralisation of an intensely personal process. Can the supposed right to have a child, for instance, really justify post-mortem conception? In the more general field of personal relations, the supposed right to self-satisfaction is increasingly used as an excuse for overriding fidelity. A distinguished writer, who had just left his wife and children, recently declared divorce to be 'morally legitimate' because it 'accords respect to an individual's needs against the devouring claims of family life.'[12] Claims to autonomy, in short, when clothed in the usefully non-religious language of rights and needs, can put on moral airs, even in the process of revealing their origins in self-preoccupied individualism.

Nevertheless to argue, as I have been doing, that autonomy by itself is not enough, is not the same as establishing that morality must have a religious basis. In fact there is a further ground, besides that of rebellion against external authority, for disconnecting the two. It lies in an ancient argument of a more philosophical kind, which in various guises has undergirded the now common feeling that religion is irrelevant to morality.

The argument asserts that, not only is religious faith unnecessary, or even dangerous, as a basis for morality, but that the two are logically incompatible. It derives originally from a question posed by Plato, who asked what is meant by saying that God wills us to do good.[13] The question leads to a dilemma. Does God will us to do good because certain acts *are* good, or is an act good only because God wills it? If God wills the good because it *is* good, then goodness must in some sense exist independently of God, and there is no need for God as the guarantor of morality. If on the other hand an act is good simply because God wills it, then to say that God is good is no different from saying that God does what he wills, which is not to say anything morally significant. Either way the conclusion seems an uncomfortable one for believers, especially those who hold the view that the moral life is essentially about obedience to the divine commands. What is at risk is not just the belief of those who loudly proclaim that better teaching about the Ten Commandments is the answer to all our social problems. The nub of the argument is the much more radical claim that obligation itself cannot have a transcendent ground in the will of God, because to identify good with God's will is to run into a contradiction. If the claim is accepted, it gives philosophical plausibility to the increasingly common assumption that morality does not need, and cannot validly possess, a religious basis, and is therefore in the last resort to be understood as a matter of personal choice or social custom.

It is worth noting, though, that the dilemma is not just a philosophical conundrum, but is implicit in at least two places in the Bible itself, where the demands of God and of ordinary morality seem to be in conflict. The first and most obvious is the story of the sacrifice of Isaac.[14] Abraham is commanded by God to do something which by every other biblical standard is wrong, yet is required as a test of faith. The fact that in the end the sacrifice is not demanded in no way lessens the sheer horror of the story in its revelation of something dark and mysterious at the heart of religion. Morality has to be transcended, it seems, when the believer is face to face with the absurdity of the demands of faith. Kierkegaard* in his famous exposition of the story makes the point that faith is the highest virtue, because it is only by faith that we can be transformed. It is only by giving ourselves unreservedly to God – not because it makes moral sense to do so, nor because we hope to gain thereby – that we can plumb the depths of divine obedience. But there remains a nagging doubt. If morality is supposed to be universal, can it really be discounted, even under such extreme pressure from God?[15]

The Book of Job provides a similar example. Here the dilemma is even more evident, because the heart of Job's anguish is his realisation that in pleading for justice against God, there is no one but God to whom he can appeal, the very God who apppears to act so unjustly towards him. 'Let not the earth cover my blood,

---

* Søren Kierkegaard, *Fear and Trembling* (1843). The whole book is a brilliant exposition of the story, centring on the question, can the personal demand of faith ever justify the suspension of the universal demand of ethics? For a different treatment of the story see Chapter 6.

and let my cry for justice find no rest! For now my witness is in heaven; there is One on high ready to answer for me. My appeal will come before God, while my eyes turn anxiously to him. If only there were one to arbitrate between man and God, as between a man and his neighbour!'[16] We are back to the question of morally unaccountable power.

For Job, as for Abraham, the dilemma began to be resolved only in a new encounter with God. In Abraham's case it was the God who provided what he himself demanded – the archetypal experience of grace. In Job's case he learnt nothing that had not already been stated in theologically exemplary terms by his friends, but he learnt it from the God who answered him. The fact that God answered at all, even though he said nothing new, was what made the difference. Job is the archetypal reminder that it is not moral and spiritual reassurance we need in the face of unjust suffering and disaster, but God himself.

The significance of the two stories for our purposes is that they open up the specifically religious dimension in what Plato presented as a philosophical dilemma. To believe in God as the ultimate ground of goodness, such insight seems to tell us, is not in practice the same as accepting a series of divine commands, as if these had been imposed by some all-powerful and morally good authority figure who merely demands obedience. The religious aspiration after goodness is a thirst for God himself, God as the ultimate fulfilment of all hopes and desires, and God as the summation of all values. The Psalmist in complaining about manifest social injustice makes the same point. 'Whom have I in heaven but thee, and there is none upon earth that I desire in comparison with thee. My flesh and my heart faileth, but God is the strength of my heart, and my portion for ever.'[17] This is far from saying that aspiration towards God carries no moral implications. The point rather is that these do not define or establish the relationship with God, but grow out of it, as in the repeated Pauline exhortation that our manner of life should 'be worthy of the Lord'.[18] Biblical morality, in other words, is not so much about obedience to an external law, as living in the light of a relationship already established by God's grace. It is an aspect of belonging and a fruit of worship. Believers should act because of what they are, and should find in God's goodness the true source of all delight, desire and devotion. Plato's dilemma is thus resolved because the recognition of goodness cannot be separated from the recognition of God himself.

But there are complications. First, our concept of God is always inadequate and may need moral correction. Secondly, the actual content of morality cannot simply be read off from our relationship with God. There are, even for most Christians, aspects of moral behaviour which may not be overtly related to religion at all, but are accepted without much thought as part of our common social and cultural heritage.[19] There may thus be conflicts between what we think we know of God, and what our ordinary moral sense tells us. The dilemma faced by some Christians concerning homosexuality is a case in point. There is also, as we have already seen, the possibility that this 'common morality' may not only conflict with religious morality, but might substitute for it.

Dostoevsky's characters asserted that belief in atheism is akin to saying that morality has no basis, and that everything is thus permitted. Were they simply being foolish in denying that there might be other sources of morality? It is now obvious, as it may not have been when Dostoevsky was writing, that a great many people with no religious belief live morally praiseworthy lives. Furthermore such people may avoid the most characteristic religious moral failings, of which hypocrisy is the most obvious. But this need not necessarily mean that Dostoevsky's agonisings were mistaken. His particular forte was the exploration of some of the deep and paradoxical springs of human behaviour. He knew that there are circumstances in which a cool rational atheistic morality is not enough. There are attitudes, insights and motives which well up, sometimes disturbingly and destructively, from the depths of our being. There can also be a constancy and a willingness for self-sacrifice, which belong only within the context of a passionate commitment. Autonomous human beings, as Nietzsche conceived them, were not cool rationalists, but needed spirit if they were to find the courage required of them.

Moral passions of this kind can easily spill over into fanaticism. But it is clear from some of the cultural disintegrations witnessed during this century that, when the going is really tough, a morality with deeper springs than common practice may be the only one to survive.[20] Dostoevsky accurately foresaw what was to happen in his own country. I vividly recall a private meeting between church leaders and the Soviet prime minister in Moscow a few months before the fall of the Berlin wall, and how he pleaded with the churches to step into the growing moral vacuum as the ideological basis of national life began to collapse.* Even atheists, when faced with a crisis of confidence, may see the need for something more than instinct, custom and social convention.

As well as supplying depth and passion, religious belief can also undergird a distinctive morality by offering characteristic and controversial insights into the nature of the world and of human life, and into their meaning and destiny. These may alter not only the tone, but also the content of moral thinking. It is the business of religion to highlight what is intrinsic to our human well-being as part of God's creation. Christian attitudes towards such medical issues as abortion, euthanasia and genetic engineering, for instance, are often distinctive, not as is sometimes claimed because Christians value human life whereas others do not, but because Christian beliefs about what a person is, and when human life begins and ends, may differ from the beliefs of non-Christians.[21] This is a further sense, then, in which common morality is not a simple substitute for a specifically religious morality. The emotional and conceptual differences between them bring us back to the point that there may be real potential for conflict between them, even touching fundamental issues.

What happens, for instance, when the insights of common

---

* This was at a meeting of the World Council of Churches in Moscow in July 1989. There is a certain irony in the fact that the last ten years have witnessed the transformation of former Institutes for Scientific Atheism into Institutes of Religious Studies.

morality challenge the deep springs of religion itself and threaten, as in Plato's dilemma, to separate goodness and God? I have been arguing that in principle this ought not to be possible because God is not a mere representative of goodness or giver of good commands; he is the very source and ground of goodness. Aspiration after the goodness discerned in God and expressed in worship, is the heart of Christian morality. It can be summed up as the response of love to the love revealed in creation and redemption. Everything else should follow from that. In practice, however, the true nature of God's goodness is only dimly perceived in the process of Christian discipleship. Loyal obedience to what are perceived to be his commands is a necessary part of this discipleship, but may not save us from serious moral dilemmas. These have to be faced as part of a never-ending attempt to understand ourselves and our world in the light of a maturing faith.

The relation between belief and morality is thus many-sided. The gradual discernment of love, and of appropriate responses to it, has entailed a constant interplay between belief and moral insights, not all of which have been drawn from belief itself, both in biblical times and throughout Christian history.[22] Belief in a tribal God bestowing special privileges to his chosen people had to give way to belief in a universal God with a servant people. The God who was perceived as commanding obedience, and prescribing elaborate rules for compliance, had to be rediscovered as a loving Father and as inner spirit, more concerned with the dispositions of the heart than with outward conformity. Job's moral argument was in essence a furious denial of the adequacy of any conception of God which implied that suffering is always justly deserved. Job was proved both right and wrong, both in the book itself and in the astonishing New Testament denouement that God himself is the one who suffers unjustly at the hands of men. The waning of belief in hell in the latter part of the nineteenth century was essentially the result of a moral perception that eternal punishment is incompatible with belief in a God whose name and nature is love. The same considerations have led many Christians to reject the substitutionary theory of the atonement, according to which the God who demands death as the wages of sin substitutes the death of Christ for the death of the sinner. There is a fine line here between suffering for sin, seen as a work of love, and suffering on behalf of others as a punishment for sin, which looks like an immoral transaction. To reject the theory is not to detract from Christ's work on the cross, but to seek to interpret a deeply mysterious event in a more morally acceptable way.

In short, Christian discernment does not start with a clear knowledge of God from which a knowledge of good and evil is then deduced, nor with clear moral insights from which current perceptions of God are judged. The two have always gone hand in hand, the knowledge of God and deeper insight into the nature of goodness interacting and mutually refining each other, so that the statement 'God is good' becomes a definition of both terms, as well as a stupendous revelation.

I have taken this rather lengthy detour through Plato's dilemma about the relation between God and goodness, because it seems to me that a theological approach to moral autonomy cannot really be understood without it. I started this chapter with descriptions of rebellion and self-assertion. I have acknowledged that there are expressions of autonomy and forms of atheism which may have positive moral value. I have also suggested that one of the reasons why moral autonomy as a ground for rejecting the Christian faith seems so attractive is that it is associated with a defective understanding of Christian morality as mere obedience, with no scope for growth or criticism. I come finally to a closer look at the concept of moral autonomy itself, and at further reasons why it is so often associated with unbelief.

Autonomy is about growing up, escaping childish dependence, taking responsibility for oneself, discovering integrity.* Religion, we are told, belongs to the childhood of the human race, when people had to be instructed what to do and how to behave,

---

* There is a curious example of this attitude in Wittgenstein's *Culture and Value* (Blackwell, 1994), p. 63e. 'I cannot kneel to pray, because it's as though my knees were stiff. I am afraid of dissolution (of my own dissolution) should I become soft.'

because they lacked the knowledge and power to make wise decisions for themselves.[23] Modernity has changed all that, giving us greater understanding of the world in which we live, and greater powers of choice. We have won the freedom to be ourselves, and to create for ourselves the kind of life we want, and it is a freedom which is not going to be lightly surrendered. 'The aim of life is self-development. To realise one's nature perfectly – that is what each of us is here for.' That is not a Nietzschean character speaking this time, but the words of Oscar Wilde at his trial. Their limitations become apparent when the same thought is put into the mouth of the essentially egotistic Lord Henry in *The Picture of Dorian Gray.* 'To be good is to be in harmony with one's self. Discord is to be forced to be in harmony with others.'[24] Yet isn't it precisely in having to face the otherness of other people that we come to know ourselves? I quote Wilde because he shows how easy it is to slip from a flippant boast or a humorous paradox into something much more deadly. Just how deadly was to be revealed in Sartre's 'Hell is other people.'[25]

It is one of today's platitudes that we depend on others to be ourselves, that life is *about* relationships, yet there is a vital difference between being gregarious and being in any deep sense open towards other people. Lord Henry did not want to be 'forced'. There can be a kind of autonomy which is not self-assertive in the Nietzschean sense, but boasts a degree of self-centredness which excludes serious relationships with others. It is fine to know people provided I can know them on my own terms, and can remain uninfluenced by them. Personal fulfilment lies in being wholly myself. Moral autonomy in this sense, therefore, is essentially about the rejection of those external demands which are experienced as stifling and oppressive, whether they come from other people or from God – but especially if they come from God.

George Steiner uses a pregnant phrase – 'the blackmail of utopia' – in deploring the pressure of the law within Judaism. Of Jesus he asks: 'Is there anyone we hate more than he or she who asks of us a sacrifice, a self-denial, a compassion, a disinterested love which we feel ourselves incapable of providing but whose validity we nevertheless acknowledge and experience in our inmost? Is there anyone we would rather annihilate from our presence than the one who insists on holding up to us the unrealistic potentialities of transcendence?'[26]

Dostoevsky, Nietzsche and Steiner, in their different ways, represent heroic extremes. For that very reason they may seem old-fashioned to those unbelievers I shall be describing in the next chapter, who reject all totalising claims in favour of individual (and ultimately meaningless) choice.[27] If life is a supermarket in which individuals can buy whatever they like, the contrast between subservience and rebellion becomes irrelevant and over-serious to the point of absurdity. For the present, however, my concern is with those who are not so glibly dismissive, and for whom there remain important questions about moral autonomy, and who want to know whether there may be a more modest version of it which is not arrogantly individualistic or heroically rebellious, and which does not have to defend itself against the all-demanding claims of God. If the effect of God's demands is simply to crush us until like Job we 'repent in dust and ashes', runs the argument, isn't it better to ignore God, and live by the ordinary standards of humanity? This is to miss the point, retorts the Christian. The demands of God are not arbitrary, they are the demands of love, the pressures put on us by one who knows us better than we know ourselves. To which the unbeliever can reply that there is no real reciprocity in this relationship with God, given that human love is only a pale shadow of what is predicated about the love of God. Love wears a different face when it is infinitely powerful. In the end it is the sense of being responsible to some external power, and being forced to do good in order to please that power, rather than for its own sake, which poisons the whole moral enterprise. It is all very well to claim, as I did earlier, that freedom in the end depends on law, but what if the law, or the majesty of the lawgiver, are out of proportion to the freedom they supposedly promise?

So the argument from moral autonomy against belief might continue, as a compelling part of the dialectic within which believers have to live. There may also be less worthy moral motives

61

for wanting to be rid of God, but these are not my concern here. What I find strange, though, about the idea of all-demanding love presupposed in this latter stage of the argument, and implied by what Steiner said about Jesus, is that love as ordinarily understood whispers rather than shouts, and respects the object of love, rather than dominates it. Baron von Hugel once wrote that 'the golden rule is to help those we love to escape from us.'[28] It is a truth which has to be discovered by every parent. It requires a withdrawal, a hiding of ourselves, for the sake of the other. I shall be considering in a later chapter how God is both known and not known. In so far as he is not known, he teaches us to be responsible for ourselves. In so far as he can be known there is a shining attractiveness, which is the motivation for worship, and it is out of worship that there arises the desire to please. I can understand what Steiner means by the 'blackmail of utopia', but I wonder what has happened to that Jewish sense of delight in the law as an incomparably gracious gift. There is a verse in Psalm 119 which for me expresses this perfectly. 'Your statutes have become my songs in the house of my pilgrimage'[29] – not a burden to be carried, but a song to lighten the journey.

If this is the nature of love, the enabling of the other to be him or herself, then it follows that moral autonomy exists for us already, waiting to be accepted as a gift from God, rather than a prize to be snatched from him. Love, if it is truly love for us and not for some abstract ideal of perfection, must want us to be ourselves, to fulfil our potential and to exercise our freedom in fashioning that little bit of the created world we call 'I'. And the more powerful love is, the greater the freedom it offers. Love must also want to be beside us, encouraging us, picking us up when we fall and releasing within us the springs of action through the awareness that we are indeed loved unconditionally. This is the doctrine of grace, the essential foundation of Christian morality. What God demands he also provides.

Secular versions of moral autonomy tend to have problems with the idea of grace.[30] There are those who have realised the need and have looked for some non-religious equivalent – enlightened education, say, to draw out natural benevolence, or the radical social readjustments which released the energies of the flower power generation, or the unflinching acceptance that this life is all, as described by David Hare. Even Dostoevsky's conspirators in *The Devils* could find inspiration in the idea of a golden age to which all their ridiculous machinations were directed. But for some even the secular equivalents of grace look too much like the dependence they have rejected. There is a fierce but mistaken pride in owing nothing to anyone.

Within the interchange of love, which is what the Christian life should be, there is room for both autonomy and dependence. If autonomy is one of the gifts of grace, then it ultimately depends on God. Yet the freedom and the responsibility are real, so real that they have eternal consequences. There is a dynamic relationship between thinking for ourselves, and allowing ourselves to be judged by what lies outside us. Just as faith and morality can grow through mutual criticism, so there are rhythms of life, from activity to dependence, weakness to strength, outward achievement and inward reflection, through which we grow in maturity as persons and become more effective in action.* Worshippers are reminded of their dependence every time they enter a church, and find themselves cut down to size, kneeling, repenting, humbly receiving, one among many, all equal before God. But it is just such a readiness to receive and to face the demands of love, knowing that we are accepted, that can restore us for active life in a demanding world. It is not a question of moral autonomy or dependence on God, but both. An awareness of moral autonomy, seized as if it were a right, is likely to find its main expression in self-assertion. When rooted in the security of God's love, and accepted as love's gift to us, it is more likely to find its expression

---

* This functional theory of religious practice, as an oscillation between auton-omous activity and a retreat to dependence, was set out in an illuminating book by Bruce Reed, *The Dynamics of Religion* (Darton, Longman and Todd, 1978). Since then it has been greatly developed and put to practical use by the Grubb Institute of Behavioural Studies, of which Reed was the founder and director.

in thankfulness and generosity. 'We love (and want to love) because he first loved us.'[31]

5

All or None

Devotees of that neglected masterpiece *Augustus Carp Esq. by Himself*[1] will need no introduction to the redoubtable Mrs Chrysostom Lorton. The book, modestly subtitled *Being the Autobiography of a Really Good Man*, is on a par with *Diary of a Nobody*, but has a more sharply defined target – religious hypocrisy. Mrs Chrysostom, after a somewhat racy past, has suffered a sudden repentance and, in her drawing-room, now stuffed with a variety of religious symbols, is explaining to Augustus, who is intent on blackmailing her, in the nicest possible way of course, that she has 'embraced religion'.

'Religion?' I said. 'What religion?'

'Every religion,' she said. 'I've embraced them all.'

'But how could you do that?' I asked.

'Oh, there was no difficulty,' she said. 'It has always been natural to me to embrace.'

I glanced round the room.

'But certain religions,' I said, 'involve the slaughter of human beings.'

'Yes, I know,' she said. 'I've included them. That's why those knives are hanging on the wall.'

'But surely you don't practise them?' I said.

'No, they're cancelled out,' she said, 'by the religions that forbid the taking of life.'

'But it seems to me,' I said, 'that, at that rate, all your religions cancel each other out.'

'Yes,' she replied. 'That's what it often seems to me.'

'But then you haven't a religion at all?'

'Well, I sometimes doubt it,' she said. 'I often wonder whether I did the right thing in embracing them?'

William James, writing a quarter of a century earlier, had a quick way of dealing with the same problem. Different religions suit different people. 'No two [people] have identical difficulties, nor should we be expected to work out identical solutions . . . so a "god of battles" must be allowed to be the god for one kind of person, a god of peace and heaven and home, the god for another. We must frankly recognise that we live in partial systems, and that parts are not interchangeable in the spiritual life. If we are peevish and jealous, destruction of the self must be an element of our religion; why need it be one if we are good and sympathetic from the outset? If we are sick souls, we require a religion of deliverance; but why think so much of deliverance, if we are healthy-minded?'[2]

James was a pragmatist, and for him the ultimate test of a religion was whether it worked. 'God is real,' he said, 'since he produces real effects.'[3] Revelations, visions and voices may authenticate particular faiths, but 'since they corroborate incompatible theological doctrines, they neutralise one another and leave no fixed result.'[4] We are faced, therefore, as James saw it, with a reality which is ultimately indescribable, but which manifests itself in different personal, social and historical forms, none of which can claim truth for itself in any absolute or exclusive sense.

The years since James wrote have only intensified the problem for believers who want to claim that *their* version of truth does not fall under this general stricture. Many have found the arguments for relativism disturbingly reinforced by the experience of living in multi-faith and multi-cultural societies. Some feel themselves drawn to Mrs Chrysostom's conclusion – the denial of all systems of belief. Philosophical scepticism about our human ability to say anything universally valid, or even anything at all, about the ultimate nature of things, rides in on the back of religious and cultural profusion. In the Western world our widening knowledge, and the growing sharpness of our critical faculties, have thus led us to a paradox. We live in an age when there is more knowledge available than has ever been available before, but the range and intensity of criticism have grown in parallel, and undermined our confidence in it. We are increasingly conscious that what we claim to know depends, at least in part, on our history, our circumstances, our temperament and the inherent limitations of being human. As with Socrates, all our knowledge serves to intensify our ignorance.

Michel Foucault expressed the point more belligerently in his phrase 'regimes of truth'. 'Each society . . . has its "general politics" of truth: that is the types of discourse which it accepts and makes function as true; the mechanisms and instances which enable one to distinguish true and false statements, the means by which each is sanctioned; the techniques and procedures accorded value in the acquisition of truth; the status of those who are charged with saying what counts as true.'[5] A regime is in effect a power structure, so the real battles about truth, according to Foucault, are not about what is true in itself, but about who has the power to prescribe what counts as true. The fact that the power of clerics has had to give way to the power of scientists, does not change the underlying dynamics. Our concept of truth is conditioned by the regime we accept as normative. Comprehensive scepticism thus seems to be the only valid response, in so far as we recognise that all our supposed knowledge is irreducibly conditioned by who, and when, and where we are.

The consequences of such notions in what we are pleased to call postmodernist culture are too evident to need much description. I shall mention just two: first their effect on our self-understanding as persons, and secondly their consequences for ethics. I shall then ask whether we are quite so helpless at evaluating different claims to truth as this scenario might indicate.

Perhaps the best place to start is with that symbol of postmodern life, the computer. Using a computer is in one sense a solitary business, as each of us sits tapping out messages on our individual screen. But within that solitude lie endless opportunities for discovering and creating one's own world, volatile virtual realities, changeable at will, understood by most users only at the level of operation on which it concerns their immediate purposes, and hence in the end dependent on the regime provided by the programmer. Linked to the Internet the computer becomes a source of limitless, unassessed and uncontrollable information, a previously undreamt of realm of freedom and power. But access to it can also threaten to overwhelm and paralyse by the kaleidoscopic variety and bewildering inconsistency of what is on offer.

Though a solitary activity, use of the Internet can also be the gateway to new kinds of relationship, through the various groups which come together for mutual support or learning, or to play fantasy games. The latter in particular can tap into feelings of rootlessness and irresponsibility. Communal fantasy games represent a form of communication by proxy, through a concealed identity. There are stories of individuals adopting bizarre Internet identities, perhaps as an amorous frog or a Roman soldier, with the aim of exploring or developing those aspects of themselves which are suppressed in life off the screen. For some the world of fantasy can become more compelling than the world of fact, with the further advantage that it can be instantly switched off, and solitude restored. The personality formation encouraged is characteristic of the kind of transient, open-ended and self-indulgent relationships which anonymity has made possible, and it is not hard to see parallels with typical postmodern lifestyles.

An American psychologist has coined the phrase 'the saturated self' to describe this process of 'colonising each other's brains . . . with the many voices of humankind – both harmonious and alien'. He goes on to describe how, as our relationships spread across the globe, and as our knowledge of other cultures relativises our attitudes and deprives us of any norm, we 'exist in a state of continuous construction and reconstruction; it is a world where anything goes that can be negotiated. Each reality of self gives way to reflexive questioning, irony and ultimately the playful probing of yet another reality. The centre fails to hold.'[6] The self, in other words, tries to escape its emptiness and isolation by becoming

68

absorbed in multiple and mostly fleeting relationships, within a game of life which has no other purpose than the formation of such relationships. It is a picture which calls to mind the currently fashionable craze for 'partying'.

The same psychologist, Kenneth Gergen, has taken this concept further in elaborating a critique of normative ethics, in which he urges the primacy of relationships over fixed principles. The Romantic notion of morality, he argues, is that it essentially concerns what is going on in the depths of an individual's thought or feelings, that it is a matter of inner intention and will. In most healthy relationships, however, people do not use this inner-directed language of rights and duties and principles, nor are they heavily introspective. They simply act in response to one another within broadly agreed conventions. It may sometimes happen that conventions have to be repaired by an appeal to moral principles, but such appeals tend to be divisive, especially when they are framed in the language of absolutes. To place the focus of moral thinking on principles, conventions and individual intentions, runs the risk of destroying relationships by creating a class of people who are in the wrong, and who therefore have to be treated as enemies or infidels. It is more profitable, says Gergen, to ask what enables people to live together in mutually satisfactory ways. He goes on, 'To the extent that whatever we hold to be "the good" in our culture is achieved through the enhancement of relationships, then it is the process of relating that deserves our closest attention. In this sense, we may confront the pervasive pluralism of contemporary life, not with dismay, but with a sense of reassurance: the very richness of patterns of relationship furnishes a resource, a set of potentials that might be absorbed with advantage into neighbouring traditions.'[7] He describes his philosophy as a constructionist relativism, the fashioning of a social, moral and intellectual reality out of a diversity which is welcomed rather than feared.

There are problems, though, with a philosophy of relationships which aims to float free from all other considerations of truth and value. These are obvious if one tries to translate the idea back into the context of inter-faith relationships. Certainly the concern with relationships as such is important; this is why there is so much emphasis today on listening and dialogue with people of other faiths, and the search for realistic forms of co-operation. But the identity of different faith communities, and the sense of security they provide for their adherents, can only be maintained if they also set limits round themselves and cherish the things which make them distinctive. So much the worse for faith communities, Gergen might say. It is this very concern for distinctiveness which has generated wars, hatred, oppression and heresy hunts. The security experienced in being different demands too high a price.

But can we simply abandon such security, any more than we can obliterate the distinctiveness of individuals? To be a 'saturated self', all relationships and no centre, is to be highly unstable, so much so that relationships themselves can be threatened. Outside the most superficial encounters, the ability to relate to other people depends on a kind of inner self-possession, what Paul Tillich called 'the courage to be',[8] a form of which I was considering in the previous chapter under the name 'autonomy'. In the growing child the transition from completely dependent relationships to relationship between equals, requires a basic attitude of trust, of having one's own place within the external world and a secure sense of the self outside any particular relationship. For that trust to develop, the first major obstacle to be overcome is anxiety in the absence of the one who cares – a theme to which I shall be returning in Chapter 7. There is also the need to overcome anxiety in the face of opposition, if relationships are to progress beyond surface platitudes. The development of a sense of distinctiveness, in other words, and the defence of it when necessary, seem to be integral parts in the formation of interesting people who might be worth relating to, despite Gergen's doubts about them. Basic trust in what we are in ourselves, and have received from others, is a condition for advancing beyond sheer defensiveness into a more complex and diversified reality.

The point is hammered home in a description by Anthony Giddens of what he calls 'pure relationships'. He describes these as free-floating relationships between two individuals, which differ from, say, traditional marriage or friendships at work, because they are not anchored in any external moral, social or economic conditions. An example might be the kind of temporary cohabitation which involves no formal obligations. Such relationships are unsupported by anything but the individuals themselves, and they exist solely for the emotional satisfaction of the two parties concerned. They break when they cease to provide this. Mutual commitment may help to buy time when things are going wrong, but the long-term stability of pure relationships depends on the extent to which intimacy can build up mutual trust.[9] If they work they can be enriching. 'Yet,' says Giddens, 'pure relationships and the nexus of intimacy in which they are involved, create enormous burdens for the integrity of the self. In so far as a relationship lacks external referents, it is morally mobilised only through "authenticity": the authentic person is the one who knows herself and is able to reveal that knowledge to the other . . . To be in authentic relation with another can be a major source of moral support, again largely because of its potential integration with basic trust. But shorn of external moral criteria, the pure relationship is vulnerable as a source of security at fateful moments and at other major life transitions.' He then goes on to explore the inner contradiction of living by a commitment within which the possibility of easy dissolution is always present. 'It is not surprising', he adds, 'that rage, anger and depressive feelings swirl through the contexts of pure relationships.'[10] The point is illustrated every week in the *News of the World*.

I have dwelt on these broadly psychological themes because I think they illuminate some of the emotional undercurrents in the condition of postmodernity. The undermining of authority, the distrust of generalisations, the affirmation of the local and particular, the multiplicity of choices, the primacy of relationships, the struggle for authenticity, the enrichment through diversity, the lack of solemnity – all these may combine to make an attractive, if somewhat bewildering, mixture within which traditional religious concerns tend to seem irrelevant and alien, when they are not seen as actively hostile. But, as I have already indicated, there are instabilities and hidden assumptions within the sort of mixture I have been describing. If emotional freedom depends in the last resort on basic trust, there is obviously more to be said about the structuring of relationships and the role of morality than appears within the rhetoric of such a transient lifestyle. Sadly, the discounting of belief is so much part of this postmodern scenario that the warnings usually fall on deaf ears. One might describe the resulting unbelief as that which follows removal of the boundaries within which religious identity is normally contained.

Whose fault is this? If the suggestion in previous chapters is correct, that forms of belief can generate their own forms of unbelief, it is worth considering whether some religious boundaries may have been drawn in the wrong way, or in the wrong places, or become too impermeable to allow scope for a more positive appreciation of what is now an inescapable pluralism.

To explore this possibility I return to the problems created for believers by the existence of a multiplicity of faiths. Treating them as equal options is, even on Mrs Chrysostom Lorton's showing, to throw doubt on them all. But the alternatives are not much more attractive. To make exclusive claims for Christianity, say, is to ignore the evidence of real spiritual depth and the positive fruits of religion in many non-Christian faiths. To claim that Christ is the hidden truth in the best of other faiths, seems like a failure to take them seriously on their own terms. The question which needs to be asked is the rather unfashionable one as to whether there is any rational means of assessing the strengths and weaknesses of different religions, and thus perhaps redrawing the boundaries between them. Do we have to accept the distinctiveness and separate integrity of each religion simply at their face value? It is a question which has wider implications, because if some kind of comparative assessment is possible in the religious sphere, then it should be possible in other cultural and moral contexts. Unbridled relativism, in short, need not be the inevitable consequence of pluralism.

I start with a famous and extreme example of religious and

cultural incompatibility, the subject of much debate thirty years ago, but still relevant, because it raised all the fundamental questions in their sharpest form.

The study of the Azande people in Southern Sudan by the anthropologist Evans-Pritchard produced a classic description of a society dominated by its belief in witchcraft. Belief in witches pervaded everything, and in particular provided the means for coping with, and making sense of, what we would describe as normal misfortunes, such as falling ill or having an accident. In the event of such a misfortune, an attempt would be made to identify which among the large class of witches was responsible, and the one identified would then be put under pressure to stop harming his victim. If he denied any involvement, recourse might be had to an oracle involving poisoned chickens, which could identify the witch with greater certainty. If the supposed witch was wise he would then renounce his witchcraft, even if he had not previously realised he was a witch, and a potentially stressful and dangerous social situation would be defused. Evans-Pritchard saw this elaborate system of beliefs and rituals as a highly effective way of exercising social control in a society where resources and knowledge were limited. At the same time he made it clear by his comments that he was aware of the falsity of its assumptions and the irrationality of its procedures.[11]

But, asked his critics, by what standard do you judge it to be false and irrational? Within the context of Azande life the pervasiveness of witchcraft as the central fact of their culture made perfectly good sense. It worked; it could be empirically verified; it made for social cohesion; and as a way of dealing with misfortune it was, in its own terms, as rational as our Western concept of luck.

The critique was launched at a time when Thomas Kuhn's ground-breaking work on major conceptual revolutions in the development of science was raising questions about whether different explanatory schemes, or paradigms as he called them, might be incommensurable, even within science itself.[12] It seemed plausible that there might be different systems of thought which are not directly comparable with one another, in that they are rooted in different fundamental assumptions, and thus cannot be logically refuted from outside their own system. The point can be made another way by asking what is meant by 'rationality' outside the particular history of Western philosophical thought. The sociologist Peter Winch put the most forceful case against Evans-Pritchard by complaining that 'he did not take seriously enough the idea that the concepts used by primitive peoples can only be interpreted in the context of the life of those peoples'; thus we cannot legislate about what is real for them or what counts as a contradiction in their beliefs.[13]

At this distance in time the opposing positions seem overdrawn. Alien faiths and cultures which may on the face of it seem naive and ill-informed, need not be dismissed as irrational. But the alternative to dismissal does not have to be complete relativism, as if different forms of rationality are only valid within their particular culture. In an earlier chapter I drew the distinction, and tried to map some of the overlaps, between explanation in the natural sciences and understanding in the human sciences – both of them rational activities. Theologians constantly face similar issues, under the label of hermeneutics, when trying to interpret for our own time and place texts belonging to times and places which, on the face of it, may seem quite alien. Some anthropologists have relied on a distinction between 'experience-near' and 'experience-distant' concepts. Experience-near concepts are what people use effortlessly to feel, think and imagine within their own culture. Experience-distant concepts are those brought from outside, to interpret the culture in terms familiar to an observer. No prior judgement need be made between the relative merits of the two, though in an anthropological context experience-distant concepts are likely to be wider and more comprehensive than the experience-near concepts of those being studied. Understanding grows through a continuous tracking from one perspective to the other.

Such tracking between different perspectives has now become a normal part of the dialogue between faiths and cultures. Each side speaks out of its own convictions and experiences, ready to learn and to identify common ground. The process initially leaves open the question whether there are rational judgements to be made between them, and thus whether it is possible to support some claims to truth above others, or to gain valid insights which occupy more than the common ground identified through dialogue. On the whole one would expect experience-distant concepts, because of their wider base and greater comprehensiveness, to yield the more convincing claims to truth, so long as they can include within themselves a sympathetic understanding of the much more existentially grounded experience-near concepts.

Alasdair Macintyre[14] has described this kind of process in a discussion of what he calls 'the rationality of traditions'. Rival traditions, confronting one another, may find their weaknesses exposed, and so begin to reformulate or reinterpret themselves. As the process continues, some of what was once believed may come to be accepted as false. Christians' beliefs about each other's traditions, for instance, and even their understanding of aspects of their own tradition, have in recent years changed radically as a result of ecumenical dialogue. Sometimes a tradition in crisis, or which has been revealed as inadequate, may find confirmation of some of its beliefs within a more comprehensive and cogent tradition, as when members of a narrow and exclusive sect begin to appreciate the resources of wisdom and experience in a broader church. Traditions, in fact, need not be closed systems, each with its own criteria of truth. In so far as there is real dialogue, and possibilities of translation between experience-near and experience-distant vocabularies, it becomes obvious that those so engaged in a process of growing understanding are not irrevocably trapped in relativism. It makes sense to talk about a deepening apprehension of reality. In Macintyre's own words:

'It follows that the only rational way for the adherents of any tradition to approach intellectually, culturally, and linguistically alien rivals is one that allows for the possibility that in one or more areas the other may be rationally superior to it in respect precisely of that in the alien tradition which

75

it cannot as yet comprehend. The claim made within each tradition that the presently established beliefs shared by the adherents of that tradition are true entails a denial that this is going to happen in respect of those beliefs, but it is the possibility of this nonetheless happening which . . . gives point to the assertion of truth and provides assertions of truth and falsity with a content.'[15]

Translating this into an inter-faith context we might say that only by allowing a faith to be vulnerable to criticism from outside, can we claim that it is true in some wider sense than simply as a valid part of its own religious culture. A recognition that this can happen within inter-faith dialogue sharpens the process enormously. It means accepting that in some matters one's own faith might need to learn from another. Such learning could only take place, though, if it was rooted in what I referred to earlier as basic trust, not to be confused with the notion that all one's beliefs are necessarily right. There has to be trust in the enterprise and its goal, mutual trust between those taking part in it and trust in what one's tradition has already delivered in terms of life-enhancement. But without the readiness to learn, and if need be to change, there is no way of establishing credibility outside the closed circle of one's own faith. This is why apologists and those engaged in inter-faith dialogue are always at risk, and are sometimes justifiably criticised for relinquishing too much distinctiveness too easily.[16]

To put some flesh on these rather abstract ideas let me take the risk of describing briefly a few of the areas in which I believe Islam tends to be more vulnerable to certain kinds of criticism than mainstream Christianity. I do so with great diffidence, and I realise that there are areas in which a Muslim might want to do the same for Christianity – not least in terms of the integration of faith into the whole of personal and social life. My aim is not to score points but to indicate the kind of considerations which could carry weight in the process of dialogue I have been describing. Such dialogue is not going to resolve major doctrinal differences but it can, as I have already suggested, expose weaknesses. I base my remarks on the work of a Muslim anthropologist, Akbar Ahmed, now a professor in Cambridge, who a few years ago wrote a much acclaimed book on *Postmodernism and Islam*.

Interestingly, none of the themes which have concerned me in this chapter – the diversity of faiths, the cultural conditioning of knowledge, the primacy of relationships over principles and the fragmentation of the self – play any significant part in his discussion. In theory he welcomes the possibility of diverse people and cultures learning from one another, but his emphasis is almost entirely on the confrontation between Islam and the Western culture responsible, as he sees it, for postmodernist excesses. He writes passionately about the Muslim sense of being beleaguered and misunderstood, and about the destructive force of the media. But there is almost no acknowledgement that there are common intellectual problems facing all religion, and that the intellectual content of Islam itself might be under threat. This absence of concern is linked with what was to me one of his most surprising disclosures. He describes how after the great period of intellectual dominance when Islamic scholars had preserved Greek philosophy for medieval Europe, Islam virtually rejected its Greek heritage and with it the spirit of criticism. He then adds, 'This rejection may help to explain the deep-rooted cultural and intellectual opposition to Islam in the West *where the ancient Greeks still matter.*'[17] The West, in other words, is blamed for wanting to learn from the Greeks about how to be rational. From the contrasted viewpoint of a Christian historian, the Muslim withdrawal from the intellectual ferment of medieval Europe is seen as a disaster for Islam. It lay in 'the sharp dichotomy between reason and will that characterises the Qur'an's doctrine of the Creator'.[18] If God's will is all we need to know, mere thinking can become impious.

These two characteristics of Islam, its sense of disorientation in the encounter with a social and political system it does not control, and its distrust of the tradition of rational religious criticism, are potential sources of weakness, just as they are for those forms of Christianity which share with Islam a desire to distance themselves from secular society and to rely on exclusive possession of an infallible written guide. Professor Ahmed has a perceptive analysis of the different ways in which Muslims react in an alien culture, and of the dangers of retreating into anger and extremism. He is aware of the difficulties Muslims face in participating in a global civilisation without losing their identity. But just as on the one hand Christians may fail to integrate their faith into the patterns of social life, so on the other hand Muslims seem not to have grasped the significance of the necessary and inbuilt tension between religious faith and any actual social order. It is not that Islam is unconcerned about social order. Quite the contrary. But unless there is also a critical element in that relationship, a critical element which for Christians is centred on the cross of Christ, the almost inevitable result is some form of absolutism through the alliance of political and religious power. It is a lesson which the Christian churches have had to learn, often painfully, but which is clearly at present much more difficult for Islam.

The fact that the Qur'an is beyond criticism only compounds the problem. The internal strength of Islam is gained at the cost of not being able openly to examine its own foundations. There is, of course, an internal logic in saying that if God is truly God then no critical examination of his revelation is possible. But it is a logic which, if pursued, cuts Islam off from any meaningful dialogue either with other faiths, or even within itself, and makes the Qur'an's own claim that it is the fulfilment of all religion viciously circular.* To put the point even more sharply, it repre-

---

* There is a sympathetic account of some of the problems Muslims have to face in inter-faith dialogue in Kenneth Cragg's *Readings in the Qur'an* (Collins, 1988), pp. 74ff. I am conscious, though, that any generalised picture of a faith, particularly a faith not one's own, is bound to contain distortions. In a lecture to the Charlemagne Institute in 1996, Crown Prince El-Hassan of Jordan argued powerfully that Islam recognises and welcomes diversity, and can thus sustain a much more subtle relationship between faith and civil society than a monolithic understanding of Allah and Qur'anic law might presuppose. In Jordan this is undoubtedly the case, but it is also probably true that Jordan remains the most Westernised of the Islamic nations. I recall in 1981 listening to a leading educationalist in Beirut bewailing his country's lack of civil society, and seeing this as the cause of many of its troubles.

sents an attitude towards religion which allows no place for the vulnerability of God and thus, as we shall see later, no convincing way of tackling the issues of freedom and suffering.

These, I suggest, are examples of weaknesses which belong within the basic structure of a faith. In some such way it should be possible to compare the structural elements of different faiths, using criteria which are not simply internal to one faith or the other. If so, there may be scope for open discussion across boundaries which might lead to actual changes and shifts of emphasis. Christians, for instance, are much more ready than they once were to learn from Buddhists about the role of meditation in exposing the limits of rational thought. They ought to be more ready to learn from Muslims about the spirituality of everyday life. Such matters are part of all serious religious practice. We are not dealing with separate closed systems, but with systems where there are overlaps, points of growth and opportunities for mutual discovery. The claims to be exploring ultimate truth are not cancelled out, even though there may be no agreed or comprehensive way in which they are seen to relate together. Inter-faith dialogue has made it luminously clear that there is a spiritual reality to be reckoned with, despite the often contradictory ways in which it is expressed. Hence it is not the diversity of religious beliefs and practices which undermines their credibility. It is the attempt to set up impassable barriers, to defend exclusiveness or to declare infallibility which, by putting everyone else in the wrong, can create the presumption that all are wrong. It only needs some very modest infiltration to reveal that God is often on both sides of the fences we erect.

If the diversity of faiths is not necessarily an argument for unbelief, can the same be said about the diversity of opinions, lifestyles, cultures and relationships, deluging the saturated selves described earlier in this chapter? The difference is that whereas all religions are in their own ways concerned with truth, and see themselves as actively pursuing it, postmodernist culture seems to have rejected the idea that truth can be known. It therefore lacks one of the essential motives which drives religions to take notice of each other.

However this is not the whole story. Part of the intellectual turmoil of our age seems to include a fascination with the idea of the transcendent, with what cannot be represented or stated, with what may be implicit in, but lies beyond the boundaries of, rational thought. Hints of the tendency to put out feelers towards transcendence can be found buried even within supposedly non-religious philosophies.[19] In my first chapter I referred light-heartedly to some of the more absurd manifestations of New Age spirituality, of which we are likely to see more in the new millennium.[20] They pose the question whether serious dialogue is possible within what I suppose we shall now have to start calling the 'spirit zone'. There is some evidence that it is, as for instance in the ground-breaking work of Eileen Barker's sociological study of the Unification Church.[21] She showed that it was possible to penetrate beneath the superficial absurdities to insights and motivations with which some sort of dialogue might be sustained. And there are other rich fields of experience waiting to be explored.★

The significant point, though, is that despite the multiplicity of beliefs, movements, cultures and seemingly incompatible ideas even on such fundamental matters as rationality, there are open and informed methods of comparing these. Whether they can lead us to what is ultimately real is a subject still to be considered. Meanwhile I feel confident that Augustus Carp might have responded less abjectly to the all-embracing Mrs Chrysostom. In

★ An informal international group, The Scientific and Medical Network, brings together scientists, doctors, philosophers and others of many different persuasions and beliefs, to explore issues at the frontiers of knowledge, which have a bearing on human existence in general and the human spirit in particular. Its journal *Network*, edited by David Lorimer, contains articles and reviews ranging from the learnedly scientific to the frankly bizarre. There are huge difficulties in trying to develop soundly based and mutually comprehensible ways of talking about experiences at the limits of human understanding. But at least the effort is being made, and there is a willingness to engage with mainstream scientific and religious thought.

a world of seemingly endless variety, the choices which matter are not between all or none, but between better or worse.

6

Anorexia Religiosa

There is a fine description in George Eliot's *Middlemarch* of how Mr Casaubon's faith in his life's work slowly withered away. Mr Casaubon, as readers will recall, was the dessicated clergyman, obsessed by gathering ever more materials for his projected magnum opus, the *Key to all Mythologies*. As the novel progresses he suffers growing uncertainty about the validity of the task and his own ability to complete it.

> 'Mr Casaubon had many scruples: he was capable of a severe self-restraint; he was resolute in being a man of honour according to the code; he would be unimpeachable by any recognised opinion. In conduct these ends had been obtained; but the difficulty of making his *Key to all Mythologies* unimpeachable weighed like lead upon his mind; and the pamphlets by which he tested his public and deposited small monumental records of his march, were far from being seen in all their significance. He suspected the Archdeacon of not having read them: he was in painful doubt as to what was really thought of them by the leading minds of Brasenose, and bitterly convinced that his old acquaintance Carp had been the writer of that depreciatory recension which was kept locked in a small drawer of Mr Casaubon's desk, and also in the dark closet of his verbal memory. These were heavy impressions to struggle against, and brought that melancholy embitterment which is the consequence of all excessive claim: even his religious faith wavered with the wavering trust in

his own authorship, and the consolations of the Christian hope in immortality seemed to lean on the immortality of the still unwritten *Key to all Mythologies*. For my part I am very sorry for him. It is an uneasy lot at best, to be what we call highly taught and yet not to enjoy: to be present at the great spectacle of life and never be liberated from a small hungry shivering self − never to be fully possessed by the glory we behold, never to have our consciousness rapturously transformed into the vividness of a thought, the ardour of a passion, the energy of an action, but always to be scholarly and uninspired, ambitious and timid, scrupulous and dim-sighted. Becoming a Dean or a Bishop would make little difference, I fear, to Mr Casaubon's uneasiness. Doubtless some ancient Greek has observed that behind the big mask and the speaking-trumpet, there must always be our poor little eyes peeping as usual and our timorous lips more or less under anxious control.'[1]

I cite him as a sad example of the collapse of a way of life from within. The burden of what has been believed or hoped becomes too heavy to bear in face of the repeated disappointment of what, perhaps from the very beginning, were unrealistic expectations. There is no longer the energy or the will to change them, so the only way to contain the anxieties is by withdrawal from the sources of life and well-being. Mr Casaubon's life shrinks as his faith in his goal, and in himself, is gradually eroded.

My theme in this chapter is starvation of the spirit, and I start with this fictional example as a reminder that there can be starvation which has nothing to do with neglect, or with the unpalatableness of what is on offer, but has deeper roots in a person's self-image and self-chosen goals. There can be an obsession with some particular insight or attitude or belief, which so distorts the rest of experience that what seems obvious to others is neglected. Later in the chapter I shall be considering two examples of such slimming down, to the point at which the Christian faith ceases to be recognisable. Meanwhile, a word about its title.

Anorexia nervosa has only come into public consciousness in the latter half of the twentieth century.* In its modern form it is a disorder of affluence, found in the kind of society where a choice of self-images is possible and where there are pressures to conform to overambitious ideals. In some it can be a means of protest against wholesomeness and normality, but it is also, more usually, an expression of anxiety, the product of fixation on an unrealistic goal, not unlike Mr Casaubon's. As such it can elicit heroic commitment and self-control in the serious business of self-transformation. The steeliness which underlies it, however, may support a wholly illusory sense of security. Those suffering from it may feel that the problems of identity, which once oppressed them, have now been mastered. Its danger lies in the almost imperceptible progress from what at first is painless, self-affirming and socially acceptable, and only later becomes a life-threatening obsession.

Religious anorexia can follow the same pattern, and for much the same reasons. The desire to revolt, peer pressure, the multiplicity of choices, self-mastery as a means of overcoming social anxiety, can all switch off the religious appetite. Unbelief gradually begins to displace belief without the need for any great crisis of faith, and in the end becomes so much part of life that any reversal of it seems unthinkable. Just as there can be untroubled religious faith – what William James described as the religion of optimism – so there can be an imperceptible erosion of faith, often hidden by maintaining some pretences, but essentially unaware of any great loss in consequence of having abandoned traditional forms of religious input.

In some cases the loss of what is specifically religious may have been masked by a change of diet. In the absence of formal religion, the spirit can feed instead on music, or other forms of art, or conversation, or nature, or whatever takes its fancy, and some of these may turn out to be quite nourishing substitutes. It is obvious

* I am told that anorexia was not uncommon among medieval nuns, particularly those who indulged in competitive fasting. But this is significantly different from the modern phenomenon.

that spiritual food does not always have to come in religious packaging. But a spirituality unrelated to a mature tradition of faith and practice is likely to lack substance, and hence to lack the standards by which to criticise itself, or the stimulus to grow beyond unreflective acceptance of what appeals to individual taste or immediate impulse. As an extreme example I think of Walt Whitman's famous lines:

> 'I could turn and live with animals, they are so placid and
> self-contained,
> I stand and look at them and long;
> They do not sweat and whine about their condition.
> They do not lie awake in the dark and weep for their sins.
> Not one is dissatisfied, not one is demented with the mania
> of owning things,
> Not one kneels to another, not to his kind that lived thou-
> sands of years ago,
> Not one is respectable or unhappy over the whole earth.'[2]

There is a cheerful complacency about this rejection of all that gives human life its edge, just as those who are nearing starvation can congratulate themselves that what they are doing is for their own good and is a cause for self-esteem. Like anorexia nervosa, anorexia religiosa is a fairly modern phenomenon, a product of cultural affluence, changing social expectations and the availability of alternative lifestyles. It is yet another example of Charles Taylor's point that the growth of unbelief in the modern period has been crucially related to the development of alternative ways of answering the intellectual questions, and fulfilling the moral and emotional needs, which previously could only be answered within a religious frame.[3] Nowadays there are endless choices and count-less role models of successful and admired people living lives in which active belief in God has no place. In that huge panorama of mid twentieth-century English life, *A Dance to the Music of Time*,[4] a Christian reader cannot help being struck by the virtual absence of any significant religious content apart from New Ageism and the occult. According to my estimate, the sum total of references are a victory celebration in St Paul's Cathedral, a funeral and a pagan dance in the woods. Most of the key characters in the novel show a strong degree of aesthetic appreciation, no religious awareness, and appetites dominated by alcohol and sex.

There is a more serious example of religious malnutrition in Bryan Magee's *Confessions of a Philosopher*.[5] In this wonderfully readable and highly personal travelogue through Western philosophy, he repeatedly castigates the sterility of linguistic analysis and its heirs, while directing attention again and again towards what he sees as philosophy's proper task – the attempt to understand the nature of reality. In contrast to Powell's novel, to read him through Christian eyes is to find oneself constantly saying, 'Yes, that's right.' Reality *is* mysterious. There *are* profound limitations to all possible knowledge. We *do* easily delude ourselves, escape into trivial tasks or reach premature and facile conclusions. But whenever he touches religious themes, Magee seems puzzlingly obtuse. The standard arguments are rehearsed, but there is none of the inner sense of what religion is ultimately about. An upbringing in which religion played no part, and in which questions about God were never taken seriously, seems to have left him without that basis in experience which might have enabled him at least to compare it on equal terms with other personal convictions about which he has no doubts. There is something missing, which he agonises about, but is unable to grasp. The appetite for it is simply not there.

In the extreme stages of starvation the ability to eat is lost and food becomes irrelevant. I think of a young philosopher of religion who recently wrote of himself 'I have never felt the need to deny the existence of God, because, for me, the idea is nonsensical, irrelevant, and antiquarian . . . if the theists who are reading this are offended by my declaration, then accept my apology, and consider this; do you ever feel the need to make a personal declaration of your unbelief in the existence of Zeus, or Thor, or Osiris? I don't think you do, for the simple reason that you find the possibilities entirely meaningless. The religions in which these gods were to be found are now things of the past.'[6] I do not know anything about the personal history of the man in question. He gives no further explanation for his view which is, to say the least, disputable, and I can only guess at what lies behind it. It would seem that he too can never have had the kind of experience, or been part of the kind of culture, which gives language about God its significance.

Not all unbelief of the kind which concerns me in this chapter follows this pattern of deprivation or slow starvation, and not all reaches its climax in such a drastic emptying out of the content of faith. Religious bulimia also has its adherents, and perhaps these can be compared to the agonised souls described by James, who pass through great spiritual crises, the twice-born, those for whom faith remains a matter of intense concern, and who move rapidly from one extreme to the other, either for faith or against it. Bulimics may have the same goal as anorexics, but they do not suppress their eating. They eat to excess, voraciously and repeatedly, and then vomit it up.

Many of the most vigorous opponents of religious faith have at one time been vigorous believers. Violent conversions, as James observed, can go either way. There is what one might call the post-fundamentalist syndrome, the sudden breaking of the dam which has held back growing doubts. In a strongly held and rigid system of belief with tightly interlocked parts, a single breach can bring down the whole edifice, and this is why comparatively minor disputes within such a system can loom so large. The collapse of an over-rigid faith is likely to be followed, if not by antagonism to what was once believed, at least by an exaggerated desire to distance oneself from it. The Epistle to the Hebrews carries fearsome threats against those who once believed and have fallen away.[7] This may seem unduly hard in pastoral terms, but psychologically it is absolutely right. The rejection of what was once believed is much more difficult to counter than simple lack of faith. The disillusioned believer wears thick protective armour. But because belief is still held to matter, twice-born unbelievers, unlike religious anorexics, cannot let it alone. They have to go on proving to themselves and others that they are not what they once were.[8]

Thus far I have been describing forms of unbelief in terms which lay the stress on its emotional and cultural undercurrents, rather than on intellectual arguments for or against what is being rejected. In turning now to look in more detail at two particular examples, I must redress the balance. There is no absence of powerful intellectual argument in those I shall be considering. But it is also clear that the attenuation of Christian faith which has marked their intellectual progress has satisfied strong emotional needs and, at least in the first of the examples, has involved a transformation of faith to conform to a particular self-image.

Daphne Hampson no longer calls herself a Christian, but she remains a theologian, and claims to be a theist, albeit of a rather unusual kind. Her most recent book, *After Christianity*, describes the point she has reached after a long spiritual journey in which feminism has played a central, though not an exclusive, role. The intellectual basis for her vigorous and decisive rejection of Christianity is to be found in two Enlightenment principles which she accepts as axiomatic.

The first, which I have already considered from a somewhat different perspective in Chapter 4, is the rejection of what she calls 'heteronomy', the concept of a God who stands outside us and over us, a law which is not that of our own being, but which confronts us and judges us. The Enlightenment was a coming of age, and its implication for her is that humanity now has to take responsibility for itself, without being dependent on, or beholden to, an external Other. The role of God, if there is one, must be to complete humanity, rather than to be hierarchically exalted over it. I quote: 'No notion of God must be allowed to disrupt the centrality of human beings (understood together, one would hope, with the rest of creation) to the picture. In this we cannot go back on the Enlightenment dethronement of God. Beyond autonomy (a falsely conceived autonomy which presupposes monadic selves) there must be a move to relationality and not back

88

to a heteronomous relation to a Christian God.'*

The tempering of autonomy by relationality (or, if I interpret her rightly, the fact that we are responsible for ourselves but should not be left to ourselves) is an important Christian theme, with which I have no quarrel. What interests me in Hampson's treatment of it is her motivation. 'No notion of God must be allowed to disrupt the centrality of human beings.' She is aware of a problem in placing oneself quite so firmly on the centre of the moral stage. Moral autonomy, important though it is, needs to be supplemented by some insight into the ultimate end of moral action and this, as Kant saw, requires an external point of reference. Thus even if we dispose of God as the prescriber of this end, there may still need to be a role for God as its guarantor. Hampson spells out this implication through her residual belief 'that the whole is in some way good or makes sense'.[9] At the same time she openly acknowledges that her argument against heteronomy is not some kind of Nietzschean rebellion, but is driven by a more personal motive – to safeguard the radically changed relationship between men and women. I quote again: 'Women will . . . wish to have an understanding of God which does not involve hierarchical presuppositions, so that God is not placed "above" human beings – even metaphorically. A woman who has overthrown a heteronomous relationship with the fathers will scarcely be of a mind

---

* Daphne Hampson, *After Christianity* (SCM, 1996), p. 11. Hampson has produced an impressive thesis, but I am intrigued by the extent to which her arguments from feminism depend on the dubious assumption that the roles, characteristics and qualities of women and men are for the most part culturally conditioned. There is an obvious motive for this emphasis if one is concerned to change the social condition of women. But it would be strange if sexual differentiations which are so prominent in the rest of the natural world, and which are clearly for the most part innate, should suddenly acquire a totally different basis in human beings. To say this is not to deny cultural conditioning, nor is it to be anti-feminist, nor is it to claim that reversals of traditional gender roles should not be attempted. It is an expression of friendly concern that some feminists should be less defensive in matters concerning biology.

to replace them with a "father" God.'* The new self-image of women, in other words, lends a degree of urgency and finality to a drastic reshaping of the image of God which goes far beyond mere changes of language. The very idea of God as the transcendent Other has to be removed from the menu because it represents the disastrous kind of dualism which has divided women and men, and made the one subordinate to the other.

Her second principle from Enlightenment thinking takes further another point I have also considered earlier, though in a different form – the dependence of Christianity on particularity in history. It is not merely that Christian origins belong to a particular time and place, and therefore suffer from historical contingency, but that they require belief in unique events which do not fit within the ordinary causal nexus. A scientific account of the world cannot cope with singularities because reliable knowledge depends upon repeatability. As she puts it, 'Whatever is the case must be the case always and everywhere, even though it should have taken until the twentieth century (or beyond) for it to be discovered.'[10] This need not imply determinism, nor need it necessarily exclude events which appear miraculous – of which she sees many, especially in relation to healing. Her point is that traditional

---

* Hampson, op. cit. p. 10. It is not only feminists, of course, who are attracted by this kind of argument. In an ironic exposition of Genesis 3 Karl Barth traces it back to the serpent's words in the garden of Eden. ' "God doth know that in the day ye eat thereof, then your eyes shall be opened, and ye shall be as gods." Therefore the grace of God does suffice up to a point, but it is not enough. God is in some sense a hard and unkind Lord. He will grant man all kinds of things, but not the best of all. He has led him by the nose in relation to this supreme good. He has indeed directed him falsely, pronouncing a threat where a promise awaited him. In effect, this state of affairs cannot go on. In effect – the serpent does not need to say it but man can and will deduce it for himself – it is time for man to be enlightened and come of age. It is time for him to . . . do a little demythologising, to pass from the decision of obedience to God to that of his own choice, from service in the garden to rule . . . Is not this a legitimate development, a necessary movement from dependence to independence, from heteronomy to autonomy, a required progress from childhood to maturity?' *Church Dogmatics*, vol. 4:1, p. 435.

Christianity depends on events which belong within a class of one. If resurrection were a repeated phenomenon, for example, then the resurrection of Jesus would not be particularly significant. But because it is claimed to be unique, it belongs by definition outside the ordinary world of which human beings are a part, and this in her view brings us back to precisely the kind of dependence on an external God which she wants to repudiate. 'I am a feminist,' she writes. 'I wish an ethical position in which I do not give myself over to any person or any God who lies outside myself.'[11]

I am compressing a long and well-constructed argument.* Once again my purpose is simply to highlight the role within it of a powerful self-image, a self-image grasped as a means of liberation. I have no wish to underrate the value of such a liberating vision, but simply to point out that because it is so central to her, it becomes the criterion by which everything else is judged, no matter how much has to be pared away in the process.

It is this process of paring away which concerns me, not feminism as such, which has played and is playing an important role in cultural transformation. Feminist readings of the Bible, for instance, can have a wonderful knack of puncturing male pretensions. I especially enjoy a feminist retelling of the story of Abraham's sacrifice of Isaac in which Sarah, with much more common sense than Abraham, tells him not to be a bone-headed fool. 'What kind of God do you think you are dealing with? What kind of God would want you to kill your own son to prove how religious you are? Don't be so stupid! She's trying to teach you something; that you must challenge even the highest authority on questions of right and wrong.' But Abraham won't listen, so Sarah

---

* There is a sense, of course, in which all events are unique. Scientists depend on repeatable patterns for the construction of scientific theories, but the assumption that everything which happens must eventually be brought within the scope of scientific theory, is an act of faith in a particular means of gathering certain kinds of knowledge, not a necessary prescription for all knowledge. Most of our knowledge of other people, for instance, is not scientific in this sharply defined sense. See Chapter 3.

advises God to send an angel in case the foolish old man continues to miss the point until it is too late.[12]

There is something very refreshing about this kind of commentary, which can often reveal further possibilities of internal criticism taking place within the Bible itself. But it is when the whole Bible and the whole of Christian theology is claimed to be so riddled with patriarchal assumptions as to be insupportable from a feminist perspective, that one begins to wonder whether the perspective itself is distorting what is being criticised. One of the most striking features of the biblical story is its dependence on paradox, its inherent tensions which have always made it vulnerable to contradictory interpretations by selective quotation. Is the God of the Bible, for example, really the patriarchal monster so comprehensively rejected by radical feminism? Or is this image only one pole of a much more subtle and complex depiction? How central to the story is the deliberate reversal of the symbolism of dominance in what Jesus taught about authority? 'You know that the recognised rulers lord it over their subjects, and the great make their authority felt. It shall not be so with you.'[13] And what kind of patriarchy is it in which children go first into the kingdom of heaven, and whose king reigns from a cross? I make these obvious points because they are not, as far as I can discover, made by Hampson. She focuses her attention instead on kenosis* as being an inadequate counterpoise to patriarchal symbolism. She points out that the self-emptying of Jesus still includes the unacceptable notion of coming down from a superior position, and thus implies hierarchy, even though it is hierarchy divested of power. But was the king in Kierkegaard's parable, who took the form of a servant to woo his lowly maiden,† really just showing

---

* 'Kenosis', the technical term for a theory of Christ's incarnation, derives from the concept of his 'self-emptying', as described in Philippians 2:7. It came to prominence in English theology through the essay by Charles Gore on 'The Holy Spirit and Incarnation' in *Lux Mundi* (1889). It has been much discussed and, suitably modified, still forms part of many attempts to describe the meaning of incarnation.

† Kierkegaard's parable is referred to in Chapter 2, and can be thought of as an earlier version of kenotic theory, though its original purpose was quite different.

condescension? Or was he revealing the true nature of love in its desire to be with the other in mutual self-giving? If this possibility of mutuality is what is meant by the declaration that God is Love, how can the symbolism of hierarchy and dominance remain unchanged? Throughout the Bible there is a breaking of symbols as well as an elaboration of them, and it is this which gives scope for the changes in perception which feminists justifiably look for, but which Hampson feels she can only achieve by rejecting the whole story, thus losing the tension which gives the Bible its constant ability to challenge complacency.[14]

There is scope, too, for a less drastic rejection of heteronomy. It is not true that the acknowledgement of God as Other necessarily implies a denial of the kind of relatedness she wants to put in its place. Might there not be a healthy element of dependence, and an awareness of a profound otherness, within a relationship which nevertheless remains supportive and affirmative? As I see it, this is what marriage should entail. To look for help from those we love and trust is not demeaning, but part of what it means to belong together. In fact it is doubtful whether one can have the kind of relationship she looks for, without a degree of dependence. Camille Paglia is notoriously wild in her criticisms of feminism, but she makes a good point when drawing a political comparison. 'Modern liberalism suffers unresolved contradictions. It exalts individualism and freedom and, on its radical wing, condemns social orders as oppressive. On the other hand, it expects government to provide materially for all, a feat manageable only by an expansion of authority and a swollen bureaucracy. In other words, liberalism defines government as tyrant father but demands that it behave as nurturant mother. Feminism has inherited these contradictions. It sees every hierarchy as repressive, a social fiction; every negative about woman is a male lie designed to keep her in place. Feminism has exceeded its proper mission of seeking political equality for women and has ended by rejecting contingency, that is, human limitation by nature or fate.'[15]

To be dependent on God as the transcendent Other is not to fall victim to some masculine plot. It is to recognise what we are as contingent and limited human beings, who are nevertheless capable of entering into affirmative relationships. This is equally true for both men and women. The fact that men and women are likely to enter into such relationships and to acknowledge their dependence in different ways and with different emphases, needs more recognition than it usually receives. I remember learning from Daphne Hampson, in the days when she was still a Christian, how women and men often have very different feelings about what they need to be saved from – men from pride and self-assertion, and women from subservience and self-abnegation. Now that she has become so antagonistic to Christianity, that balance seems to have been lost. In her much reduced theism she is left with a wholly immanent God, a part of reality on which we can draw for healing,[16] an intimate God with an attentive ear, enabling us to be ourselves by listening to us.[17] There is a certain irony in the fact that this is what Mr Casaubon wanted of his wife. But he was also terrified of becoming dependent on her for his work, because he feared that she was more alive to its shortcomings than he was. Through fear of this dependence he missed the very salvation she might have provided.

My second example of attenuated faith reverses the pattern I have been describing. Instead of having God without Christianity, there are those who want Christianity without God. Its most visible exponents in British churches are the so-called Sea of Faith group, who draw their inspiration from Don Cupitt. On the whole his disciples present a less mobile target than he does, so I begin by focusing on a slim example of popular theology by one of them, which received widespread publicity a few years ago, contained a clear exposition of a non-realist faith and led to the removal of its author from his ecclesiastical post.[18]

Anthony Freeman, a priest in the Chichester diocese, described his conversion from belief in what he described as 'a supernatural God', to the belief that religion is a purely human construction, albeit a useful one which should be preserved and celebrated. This conversion was for him a liberation from an oppressive feeling of unreality, and he saw no reason why he should not continue to

94

minister in his parish, where he claimed that many parishioners shared his view. His bishop thought otherwise.

The essence of his argument was that few people nowadays behave as if they expect God to intervene in the natural course of things, despite the language of much Christian worship. Furthermore it is not possible for the natural world to give us information about a supernatural being beyond itself. Claims that there may nevertheless be revealed truths, run into the problem that all supposed revelations betray their human origins. It is better to admit that 'God' is no more than 'the sum of all values and ideals in life',[19] and to make the most of a tradition which has managed to create some fine values and rituals, even though they correspond to nothing 'out there' – whatever that might mean.

I take seriously the idea that not having to grapple with metaphysical questions can bring relief, despite the awkward gaps this leaves when dealing with such matters as prayer, death and almost everything the church has taught about Jesus. Freeman's conversion was sudden, but followed a long period of discomfort as a Christian liberal, during which he found the use of traditional concepts increasingly at odds with his inner feelings. By giving up metaphysical assertions he was able to remain open to much of the Christian faith he had previously jettisoned, but this time accepting it as no more than a life-enhancing mythology. This, in a much more intellectually sophisticated mode, is what Don Cupitt has also been aiming to do in constructing what he has called post-Christianity, a way of life in which no metaphysical claims are made at all, but in which Christian imagery and worship can still provide a modest inspiration.

It is worth returning for a moment to Daphne Hampson who is equally shy of metaphysics, but cannot escape the feeling that there is a reality beyond us which is hard to conceptualise, but on which it is possible to draw for some assurance that our values are not wholly subjective. She quotes with approval the social anthropologist Clifford Geertz on 'the conviction that the values one holds are grounded in the inherent structure of reality, that between the way one ought to live and the way things really are there is an unbreakable inner connection.'[20]

Don Cupitt would deny that 'the way things really are' can be any different from the way we perceive and identify them through our use of language. The most we can hope for is 'a network of metaphors to help us make connections'.[21] Our world is 'a series of language formed events'[22] which can be read in different ways, and this is the only world there is. We construct our own reality.

There is undoubted truth in this. The key role of language, with all its ambivalences and shortcomings, in shaping our perception of reality, has to be conceded. But that is not the whole story. We can also think and perceive without language.[23] We regularly have experiences which are not expressible in words. Try describing a smell, for instance. Many animals clearly assess their situations and make plans without the use of words, and dog lovers can usually tell when their pets are dreaming. Language enormously refines human mental processes, but does not create the reality we perceive and respond to. There is only a limited sense, therefore, in which we construct our own reality. The ultimate nature of that reality may be for ever beyond our powers to articulate, but that does not mean that we can have no systematic contact with it, or that it is morally and emotionally irrelevant to us. It seems to me that in religious non-realism an obsession with this ultimate unknowability and inarticulacy is wrongly held to imply the impossibility of meaningful encounter with what sheerly exists. If there is any permanent value in the existentialist tradition, it must surely lie in its exposure of this error.*

The philosopher of science, Mary Hesse, has a more balanced view. She describes 'reality' as 'that to which (mental) schemas answer in complex feedback systems.'[24] The key word is 'feedback'. Nobody should pretend that it is simple or straightforward. The simple contrast between realism and non-realism obscures a much more complex and dynamic interaction. In the case of religion

---

* Martin Heidegger is unbearably difficult to read, but his great contribution to philosophy has been to force attention back to its most fundamental question – What *is* existence?

this is complicated still further by reliance on tightly knit and historically conditioned systems of symbolism which cannot be disrupted without loss of meaning. Nevertheless the fact that feedback takes place, that our thoughts answer to something, makes it possible to claim that there are better or worse ways of describing reality, and thus closer or more distant approximations to some kind of metaphysical truth.

To take a rather absurd example, in 1897 the General Assembly of the State of Indiana decreed that the value of the mathematical constant pi should be 4. It was a decision which did not do much for that state's engineering profession. But before laughing at their stupidity it is worth recalling the spoof article accepted a hundred years later for publication by a prestigious sociological journal steeped in the usual relativistic assumptions. The article was largely cobbled together from scientifically inept quotations found in the works of leading French postmodernists. Among the assertions which suffered no correction was this deliberately nonsensical gem: 'the pi of Euclid and the g [gravitational constant] of Newton, formerly thought to be constant and universal, are now perceived in their ineluctable historicity.'* The moral is that those who believe that language and culture by themselves construct our reality can end up believing anything, or nothing.

There is a parallel with idolatry. Unsympathetic critics of the Old Testament fasten on Yahweh's jealousy as the prime motive for the condemnation of idols. But there is another more interesting reason why idolatry is, and always must be, a dead end. An idol can in no way fulfil the role of God because, as the great prophets repeatedly said, 'Your own hands have made it.' Just like any mental construct, unconstrained by the reality it is supposed

---

* Alan Sokal and Jean Bricmont, *Intellectual Impostures: Postmodern Philosophers' Abuse of Science* (Profile Books, 1998), p. 210. The book is in many respects unfair, in that it picks out examples of the inept use of science in the works of fashionable French intellectuals, but does not get to grips with their main thinking. Nevertheless it successfully exposes the danger of trying to use unrelated sciences to back up dubious philosophical, sociological or psychological theses, and shows how easy it is to slip from, say, a sociological relativism into an all-embracing subjectivism.

to represent, a life-enhancing relationship with an idol we ourselves have made is impossible unless its origins are deliberately
ignored. Even the purest and most perfect summation of our ideals
must lack the qualities of groundedness, otherness and givenness,
and hence must lack religious weight, if all the time at the back
of our minds is the uncomfortable knowledge that we have made
it all up. An idol made by the self must in the end fail to deliver
because it cannot provide an external point of leverage out of the
self. But this leverage is precisely what non-idolatrous religion
claims to provide – an encounter with a presence, whether this is
perceived as challenging, affirming, healing, threatening,
empowering or overwhelming.*

In the face of such a presence, there would seem to be no need
for Hampson to feel diminished by encounter with God as Other,
if it is really true, as the New Testament affirms, that the name of
the Other is Love. Equally, it seems to me, Don Cupitt's rejection
of a metaphysical Other leads inexorably to the rejection of all
external reality, leaving only his own linguistically conditioned
stream of consciousness. His most widely quoted words in recent
years say it all: 'We should live as the Sun does. The process by
which it lives and the process by which it dies are one and the
same. It hasn't a care. It simply expends itself gloriously, and in so
doing gives life to us all.' It is a fine and moving thought – the
abandonment of all our theological, metaphysical and philosophical problems, in a life which burns itself out. No more
Bampton lectures. No more worrying about whether an argument
holds water. And, to give credit where it is due, Don Cupitt lives

* The first two of the Ten Commandments are prohibitions against idolatry, and
the theme remains a central one throughout the whole of the Bible, even
surfacing rather oddly in 1 John 5:21. There is a constant danger of the distortion
of religion through inadequate concepts of God. In fact human beings are always
trying to turn God from an ineffable mystery into a 'manageable' reality. See the
further discussion of idolatry in Chapter 7.

it. But I am reminded irresistibly of Walt Whitman and his envy of the animals.★

Neither of those whose works I have been describing in this chapter can properly be described as suffering from spiritual starvation. They are well-resourced theologians who have become contented slimmers, happy to have found ways of retaining some vestiges of a former faith. There are others, though, for whom the slow erosion of faith, not unconnected with the example set by just such theologians, is much more like the creeping despair which destroyed the soul of Mr Casaubon. For many of them the problem lies not in feminist sensibilities, nor in subtle metaphysical distinctions between realism and non-realism, but in a crushing sense of God's absence. It is to their plight, therefore, that I turn in the next chapter.

★ Cupitt, op. cit. p. 109. My criticism of Don Cupitt does not, of course, deal directly with what I take to be Freeman's more traditional metaphysical difficulties concerning God's existence. I accept the Kantian argument that God is not a subject for metaphysical proof or disproof. The essential Christian claim is that God is encountered within the practice of the Christian faith, and that it is possible to relate this encounter to other aspects of experience in rational and defensible ways. Indeed, that is the theme of this book. What is neither rational nor defensible, in my view, is to behave as if one were encountering God, or responding to the highest values, or whatever, in the clear belief that all such claims to be encountering a transcendent reality are false. Cupitt is logical in taking his language-based celebration of nothingness to its absurd conclusion. Freeman, on the other hand, tries to have his cake and eat it.

7

The Presence of an Absence

There is a saying among disabled people that what you have never had you don't miss. This is more obviously true of sight and hearing than, say, the loss of a limb or the absence of fingers. A limbless or fingerless person can observe limbs and fingers in other people, and thus be well aware of what is missing. But a person deaf or blind from birth can have no clear concept of what it is like to hear or see. The absence of an awareness of sight or sound is thus different in quality from the absence of direct experience of a fully functioning hand. It is the difference between a simple absence and the presence of an absence – an absence which is known in theory, as it were, but not missed, and an absence which is in some way felt as a loss, because the alternative to it is at least imaginable.

In exploring the presence of the absence of God it seems to me useful to start with this distinction. It is difficult to know whether there are many people for whom all religious awareness has been absent from the very start – the blind or deaf from birth in my analogy. The point was made in the previous chapter that there are certainly those who would claim this of themselves. There is also perhaps an increasing number of people in our present society who have had no significant cultural experience of religion, and hence no opportunity to develop whatever initial religious capacities they might have had. On the other hand, from a global perspective, there is ample evidence of the virtual universality of religion. Modern Western European culture seems to be a striking exception to the general presumption that religious traditions and ways of life are matters of supreme importance.

Confirmation that this European phenomenon is a form of deprivation can be found, for example, in the work of those who have analysed archetypal images in many different cultures, and have discovered enough underlying similarity to suggest a common predisposition to symbolic religious forms. One evolutionary psychologist has been sufficiently impressed by the similarities to describe religion as 'a species-specific characteristic of humankind'.[1] Another writes: 'The particular set of religious beliefs and rites practised in a given society has to be learned by each generation in the same way as its language. But the idea that there will be a religious system and a language which will have to be learned appears to exist in all growing individuals as an *a priori* assumption.'[2] In terms of my analogy with disablement, the existence of eyes and ears, even malformed ones, is a sign of the universality of sight and hearing, despite the fact that in some people these senses are congenitally absent.

My concern in this chapter, though, is mainly with those for whom the absence of God, even when the denial of him is deliberate, entails a sense of loss. This is not a modern phenomenon, though perhaps it has been felt with particular intensity during the last century and a half. The agonies suffered by the honest Victorian doubters are classic examples, as is Heidegger's 'I do not deny [God's] existence: I merely state his absence.' When Nietzsche declared that 'God is dead', he saw it as an earth-shattering announcement. This was no mere casual death. The fact that the claim is still repeated so frequently, and with such force, is a sign that the absence of God remains for many a determining factor in their lives. Even for the erstwhile Christians described in the previous chapter, the echo of God's presence still seems to be audible, despite the assumption that it must be delusive.

How and why our culture has reached a state in which it is easier to feel God's absence than his presence, is a story which has often been told, and I shall not try to retell it here.[3] I simply want to point to three interlinked features of modern consciousness,

101

which appear in many arguments for unbelief, and which gain much of their plausibility from the common experience of loss and absence which underlies them.

First there is the disenchantment or de-sacralisation of the ordinary world. Everyday life in Western culture is conducted as if God were no longer an active player within it. The explanations instinctively offered for most events, and reasons given by most people for the choices they make, seldom contain any overt reference to religion. It is customary among the literati to disparage countries and cultures in which religion is the dominant fact of life, where power rests in the hands of the clergy and where orthodox belief is the unquestionable norm. At the same time there is often a whiff of nostalgia for a now departed culture which was once so certain about where its roots lay.

Linked with this cultural change there is, secondly, enormous puzzlement about what it might mean for God to be active in the world as we now understand it. This is partly an intellectual problem, but it is also partly an experiential awareness that, apart from the occasional unexpected healing or happy coincidence, there seems to be no room for God to be active in the ways, or to the degree, that were once assumed. Miracles, on the whole, don't happen, and when they do they are metaphorical, not literal.

Most especially, and this is the third element of the consciousness I am describing, God does not seem to be active in the face of evil. I state the problem this way, rather than in terms of the familiar theological conundrum about goodness and omnipotence, because it is the practical examples of the appalling destructiveness of evil in the twentieth century which have given the question such urgency. Where was God, it is repeatedly asked, when gross injustice to millions of innocent people cried out to heaven? The sense of his absence in the multiple tragedies of our time torments many would-be believers.

But what are people actually asking for when they complain about God's absence? The fact that God may be felt to be absent is not some totally new phenomenon. The modern nexus of de-sacralisation, divine inactivity and the apparent triumph of evil, only sets the scene for the most recent version of the ancient dilemmas about this same awareness of absence. In fact there is a strong tradition to suggest that, far from being a modern aberration, the paradox of the presence of God's absence has always been part of biblical faith.

The Psalms are full of complaints that God has deserted his people. 'Why do you hide your face, heedless of our misery and our sufferings?'[4] 'God, restore us, and make your face shine on us that we may be saved.'[5] 'Lord, why have you cast me off, why do you hide your face from me?'[6] 'How long, Lord, will you hide yourself from sight?'[7] Repeated references to God's face, as representing his presence, contrast with the references to his back, which tell of his absence and unknowableness. There is the famous passage in Exodus where Moses asks to see God's glory but is told 'you will see my back, but my face must not be seen'.[8] And, most poignant of all, is the threat recorded by Jeremiah, 'In the hour of their downfall I shall turn my back and not my face towards them.'[9]

These are metaphors of relationship. To face someone is to reveal oneself to them. To hide one's face, or to turn one's back, is still to be present with them, but present as absent. God, in other words, can be known in the heights of religious awareness and fulfilment, as when his face shines upon us, or in the depths of despair or bewilderment, as when so frequently in the Old Testament he forces himself on an inattentive people by withdrawal, by bringing calamity or by overwhelming them with the dread of his holiness.

The contrast between presence and absence, God's face and God's back, may seem somewhat over-simple, but underlying the metaphor there are subtler theological concepts at work. The primary occasions when God is envisaged as turning his back are when his people are accused of idolatry.[10] As I have already had cause to say more than once, idolatry is wrong, not just for reasons of religious exclusiveness, but for the more profound reason that it is an attempt to contain God in a mental or physical structure of our own making. An idol hides God by confining him, by restricting his presence within the limits of human imagination. It conceals from its worshippers the reality of the God who so transcends all that might be said or thought about him, that his presence must also be represented by his absence. In turning his back on idolators God asserts his otherness, his absence from the very place, and in the very terms, in which he has been sought.*

Similar forms of idolatry, and similar responses to it, have occurred all through history, as for example in those self-contained and self-satisfied ways of life which congratulate themselves on being religious, only to reveal their superficiality. Nietzsche saw this very clearly. The God he described as dead was precisely this God who had been captured by a religious system, and could only be known, if at all, after all images of him had been broken. In an idolatrous society the true God may only be rediscoverable through his absence, through the emptiness of a world which is uneasily aware that something vital is missing.

There are many parallels with ordinary human relationships. One of the earliest lessons every child has to learn is how to cope with the absence of those who care for it. Without an experience of both presence and absence it can neither develop its own sense of identity, nor the basic trust in a secure reality which will enable that identity to flourish. The carer must not become an indispensable idol at the child's beck and call. That is the way children are spoilt. Nor must prolonged absence be allowed to erode all assurance that reality is somehow dependable. That is the way a child's confidence is undermined. A mature relationship is neither totally dependent nor totally independent, but carries

---

* The reasons for the biblical condemnation of idolatry are so persistently misunderstood by some critics, as if the condemnation were simply the result of narrow-mindedness, or an ancient form of political correctness, that it is worth stressing again how fundamental it is to the very meaning of the biblical descriptions of God. His transcendent holiness is such that it was forbidden among orthodox Jews even to pronounce his name. The Holy of Holies at the heart of the temple in Jerusalem was empty. Idolatry is wrong because an idol is an identifiable, and hence specifiable, thing or concept. God himself is Other.

within it a developing assurance that absence is not the same as indifference or neglect. In a word, it depends on faith in the absent one.

It is also worth noting an interesting paradox in many adult relationships, particularly in their early stages. Times of separation may allow a relationship to become more real. When people are getting to know each other, it is all too easy to focus self-consciously on the process rather than on the person, on the words being used and the mental image of the other, and on the way the relationship is progressing. Only in separation, in the presence of their absence, are we released from preoccupation with our responses to attend to the real otherness of the actual person.

There are deep biblical and experiential roots, therefore, to the belief that a sense of the absence of God need not be spiritually disastrous, and may sometimes be spiritually necessary. And there are plenty of pointers within Christian history carrying the same message. I need do no more than mention the *via negativa*, and Luther's *deus absconditus*, but I cannot resist quoting Pascal: 'If there were no obscurity, man would not be sensible of his corruption; if there were no light, man would not hope for a remedy. Thus, it is not only fair, but advantageous to us, that God is partly hidden and partly revealed.'[11]

Nor can I resist quoting some of the poetry of R. S. Thomas for whom the presence of the absence of God has been a major theme, especially in the collections of poems published in the mid 1970s. His poem '*Via Negativa*' is fairly typical:

> Why no! I never thought other than
> That God is that great absence
> In our lives, the empty silence
> Within, the place where we go
> Seeking, not in hope to
> Arrive or find. He keeps the interstices
> In our knowledge, the darkness
> Between the stars. His are the echoes
> We follow, the footprints he has just

Left. We put our hands in
His side hoping to find
It warm. We look at people
And places as though he had looked
At them, too; but miss the reflection.[12]

There are themes here which recur constantly in other poems:*

It is this great absence
that is like a presence, that compels
me to address it without hope
of a reply. It is a room I enter
from which someone has just
gone . . .
. . . What resource have I
other than the emptiness without him of my whole
being, a vacuum he may not abhor?[13]

Or again in a poem called 'Pilgrimages':

Am I too late?
Were they too late also, those
first pilgrims? He is such a fast
God, always before us and
leaving as we arrive.[14]

* An earlier tradition of metaphysical poetry, particularly that of Henry Vaughan
(1622–95), explored similar themes. Vaughan's poem 'The Night', used the story
of Nicodemus coming to Jesus by night (John 3:2) to make the point that, in a
busy pre-occupied world, darkness may lead to a truer vision of God.

There is in God (some say)
A deep, but dazzling darkness; as men here
Say it is late and dusky, because they
See not all clear;
O for that night! where I in him
Might live invisible and dim.

But night is ambivalent, just as God's absence may be. John 13:30 reintroduces
the theme of darkness in a very different context with the story of how Judas
left the presence of Jesus in order to betray him: 'and it was night'.

But in the later poems of this series he also acknowledges that watching and waiting are not enough. We have somehow to recognise God in our interpretation of events, as a sculptor recognises within the hard rock the form of the image he is chiselling out.

> . . . so in everyday life
> it is the plain facts and natural happenings
> that conceal God and reveal him to us
> little by little under the mind's tooling.[15]

There is a constant struggle to express what is not in the end expressible. So we create our images, extracting them from 'the plain facts and natural happenings', just as we ourselves are shaped in the process of articulating them. But what is this elusive reality which can be known only in 'the interstices in our knowledge and the darkness between the stars'? Is it our old and discredited friend 'the God of the gaps', the God whose credibility depends on our ignorance – the gaps in our knowledge? It is more subtle than that. Thomas is not writing about scientific or metaphysical ignorance, but about our mental and emotional silencing before the God who can only be known by reference to what is visible, but is not to be identified with what is visible. The 'darkness between the stars' is really there, but indescribable. 'The interstices in our knowledge' are not gaps which might be filled, but necessary parts of a structure which has to include its own negations. Thomas needs another range of metaphors, mostly drawn from Christ's crucifixion, to describe what *can* be known, and there was a hint of this in one of the earlier quotations with its reference to putting 'our hands in his side, hoping to find it warm'.

But what happens when we drop the metaphors? Is there really a difference between the God who merely seems to be absent, and the God whose credibility has been removed by the growth of knowledge? The strange fact that a hunger for the absent God persists, even intensifies, in an era when knowledge is exploding, suggests that it is rooted in something more fundamental than intellectual confusion. The forms of this hunger may bear little relation to traditional religious orthodoxies, but it seems that most people cannot brush aside the sense that there are things which matter, and that this mattering is not a mere question of knowledge and social convention.[16] It implies an orientation of one's life towards what lies outside it, a recognition of values which transcend the individual, and even the culture. It is as if one was being invited to respond and receive.

Within a Christian context this is familiar territory. Thomas goes on from his sense of the absence of God to ask what might be the next step for the seeker:

> To learn to distrust the distrust
> of feeling . . .?
> To yield to an unfelt pressure that, irresistible
> in itself, had the character of everything
> but coercion? To believe, looking up
> into invisible eyes shielded against love's
> glare, in the ubiquity of a vast concern?[17]

He is describing the experience of grace, the discovery that God is neither the end-product of our human seeking, nor some stupendous construction of human thought, but can only be known in his giving of himself in a manner of his own choosing:

> As I had always known
> he would come, unannounced,
> remarkable merely for the absence
> of clamour. So truth must appear
> to the thinker; at a stage
> of the experiment, the answer
> must quietly emerge. I looked
> at him, not with the eye
> only, but with the whole
> of my being, overflowing with
> him as a chalice would
> with the sea.[18]

So what is the aim of all this immense effort to articulate what in

108

the end can only be received? It is a necessary part of clearing away the false images, deposing the all-consuming idols, coming to terms with the now ubiquitous machine – a symbol much used by Thomas for the de-sacralisation of the world of nature.

> . . . looking at
> me say what time it is
> on love's face, for we have
> no business here other than
> to disprove certainties the clock knows.[19]

I have spent more time than perhaps I should on R. S. Thomas because for me, and I suspect for many other Christians and would-be believers, he has been a liberating influence. Only a writer who deals so compellingly with words can express why words are inadequate for what most needs to be said, without toppling over into that fashionable despair of language which empties it of communicable meaning. There should rightly be an austerity in language about God, all the more necessary given the stridency of so many current expressions of religious certainties, and the difficulty of reconciling them with the world as most of us experience it. But there has also to be a tight grip on the paradox of presence through absence, if the signs of God's absence are not to become the grounds for unbelief. It seems to me that R. S. Thomas speaks powerfully to these needs.

So what light can his austerity throw on the three interlinked themes of this chapter? The de-sacralisation of the world is the price paid for the growth of knowledge. The point has often been made that Western science in its origins depended on prior theological assumptions about the order, rationality and contingency of the natural world. But even when these assumptions are acknowledged, it does not follow that science or any other branch of knowledge must remain in bondage to theology. Each new intellectual discipline has had to fight for its separate existence, and devise its own categories, if it was to make any progress in its chosen field. The inevitable result has been the fragmentation of knowledge and the confinement of theology to its own diminishing sphere. From being the foundation of all knowledge, and the cement which bound everything together, it has been relegated to the margins by today's trendsetters, as a minority interest in a world from which the sacred has been banished.

The same has happened in terms of social organisation. Once it was the churches which were the primary agents of social care. In a bureaucratised society care is divided between many agencies and has to be administered according to rules which by and large, in the interests of fairness and efficiency, discount the moral and spiritual involvement of the carers. The essence of bureaucracy is its impersonality. It operates within, and helps to fashion, a depreciated and disenchanted world.

I make these points, not in criticism, but to illustrate what desacralisation is, and why in complex modern societies it has been necessary. But what is missing, of course, is precisely that sense of wholeness and personal significance – the 'mattering' I referred to earlier – which is of the essence of a religious tradition. This is why a Christian poet like Thomas has to struggle so hard to develop new metaphors which take account of this emptiness, and which challenge the triumph of the machine – 'the clock' – in the modern world, without letting go the belief, the trust, that somehow in the midst of it the presence of an absence can still be discerned. 'We have no business here other than to disprove the certainties the clock knows.' Why? Because our very humanity depends on it.

Outside such spheres as poetry, theology and art, most of us cope with disenchantment by living life in many different compartments. The bureaucrat who tries to put aside personal feeling at work, no doubt picks it up again at home. The neurophysiologist who is convinced that thought is no more than the product of electrical changes in millions of neural networks, is unlikely to treat friends as if they were just very complicated machines. The politician who can do no wrong, comes to church, one hopes, and admits to being a miserable sinner. Such contrasts are not necessarily hypocritical. To survive in a complex modern society we need to tell different stories about ourselves and to speak different languages – the languages, say, of science or technology or social administration, as well as the language of ethics and religious devotion – and to allow life to move between these different poles, making connections where possible and drawing strength through an honest facing of personal limitation and failure.

Religious ritual at its best can create the context for this to happen, by offering a secure means of journeying inward to the damaged self and its relationships, and then outward again to a world newly seen as a sphere of moral action.* The rediscovery of the power of meditation, and the growth in the number of those going on retreat, are among the many signs of the widespread hunger for, and the possibility of, some kind of wholeness. We need a garden, away from the busy world, in which to catch up with our souls. Thomas uses the same metaphor and adds his own resonances to it. After describing himself as having 'come to the borders of the understanding', he addresses God:

> . . . Call your horizons
> in. Suffer the domestication
> for a moment of the ferocities
> you inhabit, a garden for us to refine
> our ignorance in under the boughs of love.[20]

Art, poetry, meditation and ritual may help us to cope on an emotional level with the fragmentation of a de-sacralised world without losing our souls, but they do not take us far into the intellectual problem of how God's activity in the world might be conceptualised. The presence of an absence may be felt and responded to, but does it actually make any difference to what happens?

---

* This theory of religion has already been referred to in the note on p. 63. It is based on the concept of oscillation between dependent and independent states of mind. According to it, the psychological role of religious ritual is to allow worshippers to acknowledge feelings of dependence, unworthiness, etc., and by bringing them into relationship with redemptive and empowering love, to turn them round to face the world again.

The simplest and most obvious answer is that if we as human beings, through exercising our intentions, can make a difference to what happens, then there ought not to be a problem in imagining how God might do the same. If God is the ultimate reality, creating all things and holding them in being, and if his steadfast will is what we experience as the regularities of nature, there is no *a priori* reason to suppose that, within these regularities, there might not be occasions for his intentions to be experienced more directly and less predictably. The denial of such freedom to God is no more, and no less, logical than the denial of free will to human beings. The difficulty is that, whereas it is possible to observe human beings at least appearing to act freely, and believing that they can indeed 'disturb the universe',* it is much harder to pinpoint, or even to imagine, the free action of God without it seeming to be gratuitous interference. Furthermore if he really does act freely, we are then confronted with the nightmarish question of why, in the face of evil, he does not act more frequently.

It seems to me that these difficulties might look less fearsome if we were to think of God's freedom to act as being not only analogous to, but inextricably linked with, our own freedom to respond to his presence. If there is already, as it were, an openness in the fabric of reality where human intentions can operate, then faith in God, and empowerment by him, can exploit this openness. It can alter the course of history – as it undoubtedly has – even though historians, in seeking to account for what happens, might feel no need to look beyond human actions and motivations. I am suggesting, in short, that at the very least and as a basic minimum, it is possible to identify a potential creativeness in the

---

* The phrase is from T. S. Eliot's 'The Love Song of J. Alfred Prufrock', and was used by the theoretical physicist, Freeman Dyson, as the title of his book *Disturbing the Universe* (Harper and Row, 1979). The point is that even the Prufrocks of this world may dare to 'disturb the universe'. The book is full of sensitive reflections on the practical exercise of freedom in a culture empowered by science and technology to change the way things are. Each of us can, and does, make a difference.

relationship with God or, to put it more vaguely, in openness to the transcendent, which can effect change but cannot be captured within the ordinary category of material causality.

There are some obvious objections to any such claim. Is God's freedom to act really limited to what he can do through human beings? Are we not being absurdly anthropocentric in assigning this role to such insignificant latecomers within the aeons of the universe's existence? The answer is that we do not know how God might be present in the rest of the natural world and in lives of which we can have no inner knowledge. Nor can we penetrate beyond our categories of space, time and causality, to whatever reality manifests itself through them.* Our knowledge of God, such as it is, rests on events which we interpret as his dealings with us, and these do seem to follow the pattern I have been describing. They constitute, in Thomas's words, 'an unfelt pressure that, irresistible in itself, [has] the character of everything but coercion'. Yet this uncoercive pressure from omnipotent love is not directed towards us alone, but belongs within 'the ubiquity of a vast concern'. There is no need for us to think of ourselves as the only channel of this vast concern, but we are the only channel of which we have direct experience.

Seen in these terms, the presence of God's absence represents his determination not to coerce but to evoke, to work in and through his creation by allowing it to be itself, and to disclose its meaning as the sculptor finds the shape emerging from the hard rock 'under the mind's tooling'. Much of the Bible can be read as an account of this kind of interaction in which, on the human side, the faithful response to what is at first only dimly perceived, is the driving force behind extraordinary events. The Jews' return from exile in Babylon is one of the classic examples of prophetic faith animating a dispirited people to do what, without it, they

---

* The reference here is to the key insight of Kantian philosophy, namely that all human experience is an interpretation, through the categories of space, time and causality, of an otherwise unknowable reality.

would have judged impossible.* The persistent biblical theme of promise and fulfilment weaves its way through history, enabling one fulfilment to build on another. It could even be said of the incarnation that it is the supreme and definitive example of God's purpose in willing to act through human agency.

A more fundamental objection to what I have been suggesting about this mode of God's activity is that it might seem to make God himself redundant. If response to God is the operative principle, and if the works of God are done primarily through human beings, and if for the sake of argument we discount the significance of the incarnation, is there any difference in practice between faith in a real God and faith in an imaginary one? Might not the thought of God be just as empowering as his actual presence? We met this same objection in the last chapter. In its developed form it goes back to Feuerbach's recasting of the whole of theology as anthropology.† A major problem with it is that if the objection is acknowledged as valid, faith ceases to be effective. To have a relationship with a God known to be imaginary is neither to be inspired nor empowered, for one is knowingly basing one's life on an illusion. Living one's life for God necessarily entails believing that some, at least, of what is said about him is true. Note that this is not an argument for the existence of God; it is an argument against the claim that, if God is understood as working through

---

*The prophecies of Deutero-Isaiah (chs. 40–55), and probably also parts of Ezekiel, almost certainly provided the stimulus to Jewish exiles in Babylon to make the dangerous return to Jerusalem. The belief that God was unique, universal and in control of their history made it possible for them to uproot themselves from the relative security of exile within a great empire. The belief fed on the prior belief that an earlier generation had been rescued in a similar fashion through the exodus from Egypt. It is significant, though, that God was also perceived as working through those who did not consciously acknowledge him, e.g. Isaiah 45:1–6.

† Ludwig Feuerbach's *The Essence of Christianity* (English translation, 1854) is commonly regarded as one of the foundation documents of nineteenth-century humanism. He 'explained' religion as being essentially about the highest hopes and thoughts of human beings, rather than about any metaphysical reality. Marx was much influenced by him.

the exercise of human freedom, it makes no difference whether he is real or imaginary. On the contrary, it is precisely the awareness of being called to transcend oneself by a reality beyond oneself that makes faithful and heroic action possible. The essence of faith is response, not invention.

William James gave credence to religious experience because it works, it changes lives. I have already quoted his 'God is real since he produces real effects'.[21] There has been much argument ever since about whether this kind of pragmatism can provide an adequate criterion of truth. Probably not. False beliefs can for a time be highly effective. But the 'real effects' of God do seem to point to something permanent, not least in those many examples of conspicuous sanctity to be found in virtually every faith. Religion itself remains impressively persistent. There is a winnowing process in history which in the end exposes deception, but which has not managed to blow away the core of religious awareness I have been trying to describe.

If the mode of God's action in the world really is to be understood as hidden within natural processes, including the exercise of human freedom, the third and greatest of the dilemmas confronting faith might begin to look less threatening. The mystery of evil remains impenetrable. R. S. Thomas calls on God to 'Suffer the domestication for a moment of the ferocities you inhabit' – the word 'ferocities' conjuring up the sense of danger, the dark energy lurking in the background of much religion and manifest in some of its more violent expressions. But this gives way immediately to 'a garden for us to refine our ignorance in under the boughs of love'. In fact it is two gardens – one where the knowledge of good and evil was deliberately chosen in preference to ignorance, and one where love made its choice to hang on a tree.★

The reality of our choosing between good and evil gives special point to the idea of God acting against the world's evils and

★ Compare Gen. 3 and Mark 14:32–42. There was temptation in both gardens, but the responses were very different. St Paul developed the contrast in Rom. 5:12–19.

sufferings through our responses to him. Christians have always recognised that, while there may be no convincing theoretical answer to the problem of evil, there can nevertheless be practical answers to particular evils, inspired and empowered by love's conquest of evil on the cross. Grace, God's gift to us of what love requires, can enable even deeply flawed human beings to turn tragedy, if not into triumph, at least into something less dark and hopeless.

Attempts to deal with the theoretical problem of evil have always focused on descriptions of what a world in which freedom is possible would have to be like. Thus 'creation is the act whereby God generates the capacity to be free from crushing omnipotence,' says one writer,[22] in a familiar exposition of evolution as God's way of letting the created universe be itself. Likewise Jürgen Moltmann, in *God in Creation*, draws on the kabbalistic tradition of the self-limitation of God. 'God makes room for his creation by withdrawing his presence.'[23] The presence of God's absence, in other words, allows creation to hint at its creator, and gives it the freedom to go its own way – but at a cost. It is an approach to the problem of evil through a theology of creation, which correlates well with recent scientific insights into the conditions necessary for a combination of creativity and stability.

One of the most fascinating conclusions from the new sciences of chaos and complexity is that complex lifelike systems can be spontaneously generated on the boundary where a stable system is just tipping over into a chaotic one.[24] These are essentially mathematical theories, but the same result might have been predicted from evolutionary history. The driving force in evolution has usually been the breakdown of stable environmental conditions in directions which, for those creatures involved, are unpredictable and life-threatening. It could be said that, biologically at least, danger is the spur to creativity. In more recent years the earth itself has been revealed as much more dependent on dynamic processes, including cataclysms and volcanic eruptions, than anyone previously suspected. To maintain a habitable environment, our world has had to go through a constant process of seemingly

116

destructive change, and the same forces are at work today. Creativity and stability, it seems, necessarily have their dark side in chaos and destruction – Thomas's 'ferocities' – just as life presupposes death. The second verse of the Bible implicitly acknowledges the reality of chaos and boldly includes it within the creative activity of God.*

These are no more than pointers to the character of creation. Critics may complain that the costs are too high. I said earlier in discussing the difference between a real and an imaginary God that we might for the sake of argument discount the significance of the incarnation. But in the face of evil and suffering that is, of course, what no Christian can do. It is precisely the fact that God, in letting the world be what it is, makes himself vulnerable to it, which changes our perception of the cost and consequences of his refusal to coerce us. Some may look in awe and perplexity at the agony in the garden and be riven by the fear that this is a God-forsaken world.† But for Christians the absence of God from that other garden where bewildered believers had hoped to find him, has never been the end of the story 'under the boughs of love'.

* Gen. 1:2. The reference in this verse is almost certainly to the ancient Baby-lonian creation myth according to which the world was fashioned out of primitive chaos. The biblical writers subordinate this idea to the overarching claim that God is the creator of everything, but the notion of primitive chaos does not completely disappear, presumably because it is too deeply rooted in experience. Nietzsche, also, ascribed creativity to chaos within. See page 48.

† The imagery of the garden in Thomas's poetry includes both Gethsemane and Eden. Trees have a similar ambivalence, and occur frequently with the double connotation – the tree of the knowledge of good and evil, and the tree of crucifixion. See, for example, 'The Tree' in R. S. Thomas, *Later Poems* (Macmillan, 1983), p. 187. The third garden contained the empty tomb, whose very emptiness provides a new symbolic twist to the idea of transcendent presence. Compare note on p. 104. The rending of the veil of the temple (Mark 15:38) at the time of Jesus' death may indicate a further symbolic link between the empty temple and the empty tomb.

117

8

Believing in Belief

'I do not believe in Belief', wrote E. M. Forster in the opening words of his once famous essay on 'What I Believe'.[1] It was written in 1939 at a time when he was understandably full of fears about the prospect of militant creeds leading the world into war. 'Tolerance, good temper and sympathy are no longer enough in a world which is rent by religious and racial persecution,' he wrote, so 'they want stiffening,' he went on, 'even if the process coarsens them. Faith, to my mind, is a stiffening process, a sort of mental starch, which ought to be applied as sparingly as possible. I dislike the stuff.'

His novels had already made clear his distrust of power, causes and authorities, all of them, as he saw it, inseparable from faith systems, and all of them potential threats to people's ability to relate authentically to one another. It was the priority of personal relationships which lay at the heart of his own creed, and which provoked his notorious remark about hoping he would have the guts to betray his country rather than betray his friend. The preference might look somewhat different if expressed by a politician instead of by a novelist, but he enjoyed the luxury, like many of those renowned for their outspokenness, of not actually carrying any public responsibility.

Forster gave two cheers for Democracy, 'one because it admits variety and two because it permits criticism'. In his opinion only 'Love the Beloved Republic, which feeds upon Freedom and lives' deserved three cheers. He also believed in 'an aristocracy of the sensitive, the considerate and the plucky'. Christianity he saw as unable to cope with 'the present worldwide mess' because it had lost its spiritual force. His was a small faith, all that was left to 'an individualist and a liberal who had found liberalism crumbling beneath him'. But he saw other people's faith as equally insecure. A modest belief might be needed to see one through hard times, but dogmatic belief was for him the antithesis of his most precious values.

In the immediate aftermath of the war another, much less famous novelist, Nigel Balchin, expressed a similar mood of disaffection with causes, creeds and the tub-thumping certainties of those who knew exactly where they were going in life. He called his book *Lord, I was Afraid*, a reference to the servant with one talent in Jesus' parable, who went and buried it in the ground. The novel ends with a long speech by the central character who is about to drown in an updated version of Noah's flood.

> 'We stood at a crossroad of time, with all the signposts down. We saw error and ignorance and prejudice and stupidity go marching boldly down the roads away from somewhere and towards anywhere. The bands were playing and the flags flying. It would have been easy to follow. But we stood there, fumbling for our lost compass and our missing map – waiting for the stars to come out and give us a bearing; waiting until it was light; and in the end waiting because we had always waited. That was our failure. And we must drown for it. Yes, yes, we know. We have no complaint, and ask no mercy. It is for God to decide what sort of man He wants, and He has always had a partiality for the stone-slinging, ruddy-faced sinner who could slay you his ten thousands, and come straight home to a bout of hearty adultery, and then weep in his bed of repentance. But Michal, Saul's daughter, despised him in her heart, and so do we. We have slain no Goliaths, but Uriah's blood is not on our hands. We may be nothing, but at least we are not the Practical Man – the Realist – the Fixer . . . Lord, I was afraid, and went and hid thy talent in the earth; lo, there Thou hast that is Thine.

Unused, unincreased, unvalued; unenjoyed; unlost, undirtied, untarnished, undebased; for what it's worth. . . .'[2]

I have quoted these two because, although they belong to an era long past, their expression of the world-weary temper which wants to cultivate its own garden and to dispense with all but very tenuous belief, can still resonate with our own times. They represent two versions of an aesthetic distaste for religion, of a kind nowadays generally found on the Arts pages of our broadsheets. In Forster's case it was a Bloomsbury-like sentiment that it is vulgar to believe in anything but high culture and friendship, and in Balchin's a 'been there, done that' imputation that religion is finished, and is in any case too readily exploited by the militant and the self-obsessed. Since they wrote the world has seen some unexpected, and to many people rather embarrassing, revivals of dogmatic religious movements. Nevertheless the prevailing culture of the Western world, both in the arts and the sciences, continues to entertain a deep suspicion of the idea of belief itself. The fragile, individual, tolerant and person-centred values which Forster celebrated, not only survived the violence he so dreaded, but went on to provide the basis for a kind of civilised decency, making minimal claims on any overt profession of faith. They are now once again threatened by the stronger forces of self-assertive individualism.

The withdrawal from life, described by Balchin, also has its modern parallels, though perhaps in not quite such a negative and anxiety-ridden form. The maxim 'rather make nothing than make a mistake' has become, 'do what you will, and believe what you will, for nothing really matters provided you do no harm. Live for the present. See that life is absurd, and accept that all commitment is arbitrary.' I was struck recently by a comment attributed to the actor Stephen Fry in an interview for a Sunday supplement, which falls into this category. He is quoted as saying of himself: 'I don't want to be fixed in what I think. I'd like to believe that next year I'll believe nothing I say today, and everything I thought today I might think differently about.'[3] Give or take a bit for the silly things people say when they are being interviewed, it is still by any standards a remarkable statement. If he meant it, he was implying no continuity between the self he is today and the self he might be tomorrow. If he didn't mean it, he was implying no continuity between what he said yesterday and what he is saying today. Taken at face value, it is so fully to equate belief with transient feeling as to threaten the very notion of personal identity.

These are extremes and, as we have seen, even Forster in disavowing belief went on to express a modest faith. But the culture of not believing is real enough, and my aim in this book has been to expose some of its roots.

One of these is the widespread assumption that any profession of faith, particularly religious faith, must be irrational. The most radical claim is that there is no rational way of answering any of the fundamental questions about the ultimate nature of things, or even about reason itself. If Kant and his successors are not enough to convince anyone who doubts this, the irreconcilable differences between those who profess to have answers are held to be sufficient to prove the point. The assumption of religious irrationality is further reinforced by the observation that many beliefs clearly are irrational, and some of those who hold them take pride in the fact and regard it as a sign of their divine origin. I recall a conversation with a young Israeli whom I was questioning about the strict separation in orthodox Jewish practice between foods containing milk and those containing meat. I reminded him of its apparently irrational origin in an obscure command in what were probably pre-Israelite laws.[4] His reply was direct and disarming. 'What would be the point of believing in a God who never asked you to do anything which might appear unreasonable?'

There is a style of religious apologetic which goes even further. While admitting its dependence on a faith which cannot be rationally proved, it goes on to claim with some justice that every other branch of knowledge faces the same dilemma. The reason why rational and intelligent people differ in their philosophical beliefs is that there is no non-arbitrary way of choosing one's basic assumptions. Theology, therefore, has just as much right to make its absolute claims as sceptical philosophy, in fact more so because its fundamental insights are not arbitrary, but have been revealed in sacred history. It is the kind of riposte which is still popular in some neo-orthodox theological circles, and it forces attention to what is actually meant by being rational. But the riposte fails if the criterion of rationality, instead of involving adherence to – and logical construction on – unassailable foundational principles, lies in the ability to withstand criticism.*

I have returned repeatedly in previous chapters to the point that religious belief has to be in dialogue with other forms of knowledge, and that its claim to rationality depends on the integrity of this process. This is not to say that all knowledge is of the same kind, and that all evidence must necessarily meet the same standards. In commending the distinction between explanation and understanding (Chapter 3), in accepting that there is an inevitable degree of pluralism in all approaches to God (Chapter 5) and in acknowledging the severe limitations in our knowledge of God (Chapter 7), I have nevertheless been concerned to stress that critical evaluation is possible, and has been a constant factor within Christian history. Faith is tested by the experience of living, and while nobody can deny that there have been appalling failures and disappointments, it is also true that triumphs of love, sanctity, vision, creativeness, endurance and ordinary goodness, witness to an essential rightness at the heart of it.

If we are to be properly critical, though, there has to be some

---

* This general thesis is well set out in W. W. Bartley, *The Retreat to Commitment* (Chatto and Windus, 1964). At the time Barthian theology was regarded by many theologians as having provided an unanswerable response to rationalism. Bartley drew heavily on the philosophy of Karl Popper for whom the ability to withstand criticism was the basis of all knowledge. In the political sphere there is a nice analogy with democracy. Popper makes the point that it is possible to have a democratic system which leaves unanswered the endlessly disputable questions about the sources of authority, provided there is a satisfactory means of getting rid of bad rulers or restricting the harm they do. See Karl Popper, *The Open Society and its Enemies* (Routledge, 1966), p. 121. Nevertheless, as the failure of many modern democracies has revealed, the power to criticise and the ability to accept criticism do in practice depend upon some prior values being held by the people concerned. The same is true, I suspect, in philosophy.

criterion of what counts as valid criticism, and that may be as difficult to define as the attempt to lay down solid foundational principles. The fact is that, despite intensive criticism, rational people can continue to differ on quite fundamental matters and find themselves unable to resolve their differences. Why else would there be different schools of philosophy, for instance? The answer seems to be that it is often impossible for criticism to reach those unstated, and usually inarticulate, insights which make different beliefs and assumptions seem plausible to those who hold them. Usually it is only the passage of time which exposes them, and that is why one needs the long view of traditions, and of those insights which have survived for millennia, as well as a certain scepticism towards passing intellectual fashions. A less demanding alternative might be to identify what ought to count as invalid criticism, and I have an example to hand.

In a famous essay on *The Ethics of Belief*, the nineteenth-century philosopher W. K. Clifford laid down a principle which has been widely quoted ever since, usually to the detriment of religion. 'It is wrong always, everywhere, and for anyone', he wrote, 'to believe anything upon insufficient evidence.' Here, it might seem, is a clear basis for rational criticism. Clifford was not overtly writing about religion, and the universal form in which he stated his principle implies that it should by no means be confined to religion. Nevertheless a perceptive philosopher has remarked on the curious fact that his principle 'is almost never mentioned except in hostile examinations of religious belief and . . . the anti-religious writers who mention it never apply it to anything but religious beliefs.'[5] The reason is not far to seek. If a critical principle of this severity were to be applied to the rest of life the results would be devastating. Freud would have died an unknown physician in Vienna. Beef on the bone would become an even more distant dream. Newspapers would have to be classed as fiction. Politicians would be silenced, and all philosophers would necessarily have to become agnostics. The word 'evidence' seems on the face of it to be hard and clear, to apply only to the kind of material which can be observed with scientific instruments, or found in sworn testimonies. It belongs to a specialist market in which religions find it hard to compete. In practice, though, everybody relies on, and lives by, countless observations, insights and personal judgements which come nowhere near this level of evidence. So why when Clifford's principle is applied to religion, does it suddenly and unaccountably begin to operate with full rigour? Religious claims may sometimes seem remarkable but, *pace* Hume, that is not a justification for requiring them to pass evidential tests which would seem ludicrously excessive in most other areas of life.

The criteria for valid criticism become even more complex when it is realised that the purpose of many statements of belief is not so much to convey direct information, as to keep the door open to what can only be stated paradoxically. The doctrine of the Trinity, for instance, is not an exercise in divine map-making, as if one could somehow penetrate the mystery of God's own being. Its function is to define the boundaries of thinking about God, and constantly to redirect attention to the complexity of the historical experience on which knowledge of God is based. The crucial question to be asked about such beliefs is how well they withstand the criticism which is appropriate to their subject matter, and which takes account of the type of evidence it might be reasonable to expect. That in turn requires an understanding of why particular beliefs have taken the form they have as part of a total way of life. The dismissive use of the word 'irrational' is generally much too blunt an instrument to use in such a complex exercise. Christian believers should not allow themselves to be intimidated by it, especially when it relies on hostile caricatures of subtle theological constructions.

Among other factors which contribute to what I have earlier called 'the culture of unbelief' is bewilderment at the pace and scale of change. Awareness of God was once such a natural and central part of the public frame of reference, that a great variety of religious claims and activities could be simply taken for granted, much as we now take for granted the regularities of nature. Serious challenges to a frame of reference can start a

124

landslide, because people's basic assumptions are usually the ones
for which they have not learnt any reasons. It can be extraordinarily difficult suddenly to have to defend one's instinctive or
lifelong beliefs, and when reasons for them are hurriedly sought
these can sometimes look frighteningly unconvincing. How does
one start to prove to a determined opponent, for example, that
love is the supreme value? The vulnerability of some deep-seated
beliefs to unexpected challenges, though, does not mean that no
good reasons for them can be found. Nor need they necessarily
be abandoned, any more than belief in causality has to be abandoned as a guide in ordinary life, just because David Hume asked
awkward questions about it.*

Much of religion hovers on the edge of inarticulacy. What can
be said falls short of expressing and conveying what can only be
known in the process of experiencing it. Hence my earlier
emphasis on myth, ritual and symbolism. Traditions which are
forced to articulate and rationalise their beliefs in a hostile environment, are bound to do so inadequately, thus generating controversy
within themselves, and appearing vulnerable even to their own
adherents. The sense of God's presence, once virtually universal
and, if the research on religious experience is to be believed, still
extraordinarily widespread, now has to compete against innumerable alternative descriptions and explanations. These can appear
all the more compelling as adequate resources for expressing any
direct experience of God are depleted by ignorance of the necessary resonances in religious language.[6] Thus a whole way of
thinking and experiencing can be lost by being deprived of the
context of community, language and activity in which its significance once found expression. One of the lessons of history is that

---

* Hume's most memorable contribution to philosophy was his demonstration
that a causal connection between events cannot be directly observed nor can it
be logically deduced. All that it is possible actually to observe is that one thing
regularly follows another – what he called 'constant conjunction'. It was this
claim which led Kant to formulate his seminal insight that space, time and
causality are not realities 'out there', but categories in terms of which human
beings interpret an otherwise unknowable reality.

some religions die, though more, I suspect, as the result of cultural change than through intellectual collapse.

I see a third element in the culture of unbelief as the ever-increasing fragmentation of knowledge, and the consequent fear of seeming foolish in a world dominated by expertise. A sentence in one of Monica Furlong's early books has long stuck in my mind. 'In a world of experts everyone becomes afraid to know anything, even the things they do know.'[7] She was actually writing about motherhood, but the words could apply equally well to theology. What ought to belong to everybody, and is rooted in everybody's knowledge of life, becomes a matter for experts only. The rows of theological books in the libraries of great houses may not have been much read by their owners, but their presence testifies to the fact that theologians once wrote for a general readership. In a world swamped by expert knowledge that could not continue. I have the greatest respect for the difficult job faced by today's professional theologians in a highly competitive and critical academic environment. Unfortunately there is a price to pay for it in terms of comprehensibility. Religion, like every other subject, has become a specialist interest. Many of those who might have something to say feel inhibited, while public debate on issues of belief, such as it is, tends to fall into the hands of a small number of self-publicists who have made themselves accessible to the media.

The state of religious book publishing illustrates the same point. Thousands of titles are produced every year, but it is rare, for instance, for a theological book to be reviewed in a daily newspaper, unless it makes some outrageous claim. Compare the space given to books on popular science and occultism in most non-specialist bookshops with the pathetic amount allocated to serious books on popular theology. The sad conclusion is that without the stimulus of intelligent public debate on theological matters, the culture of unbelief must become more deeply entrenched, and those who might have had the courage to express their convictions will feel bereft of support.

A fourth feature of this culture, perhaps both a consequence and a cause of it, is the retreat into private religion. There is no need to expand on this point, because the process has been described many times. It extends from Rousseau through Romanticism to our modern preoccupation with self-fulfilment.[8] There is a sense in which religious belief is in large measure necessarily inward, and in various ways highly personal, or even idiosyncratic. But the looser an individual's affiliation to some system of meaning, the more fragile personal belief is likely to be, and the less it will be open to constructive criticism. In privatised religion the line between rational belief and fantasy becomes harder to draw, thus making it easier for hostile critics to dismiss the whole of it as fantasy, and for those not averse to fantasy to indulge themselves in it more recklessly. It is said that religion flourishes under adversity, but I am not sure that includes the kind of spiritual and intellectual deprivation I have been trying to describe.

Against this generally dismissive background, the things Forster identified as distasteful about Christianity – 'poor talkative little Christianity' as he called it – were mostly of an aesthetic kind. He disliked its censoriousness and asceticism, its concentration on sin, rather than on the release of natural goodness. He asked for less chastity and more delicacy – and got one without the other. His lawgivers were Erasmus and Montaigne, not Moses and St Paul. Yet he knew how easily the cultured and rather introverted world to which he belonged could collapse into meaninglessness. In *A Passage to India*, Mrs Moore's frightening experience in the Marabar cave amounted to just such a collapse, as the terrible soulless echo in the cave undermined her hold on life. 'Pathos, piety, courage – they exist, but are identical, and so is filth. Everything exists, nothing has value,' the echo seemed to say.[9] Forster's own most precious value, the authenticity of relationships, was to be threatened in 1939 by unimaginable violence, and is threatened more subtly in our own day by new pressures to manipulate, objectivise, deconstruct, trivialise and explain away. A culture of unbelief adds sharpness and urgency to his further question: where today does one look for the spirit?

There is a revealing passage in his description of a Hindu

ceremony in which there had been striking and violent manifestations of ecstasy: 'the human spirit had tried by a desperate
contortion to ravish the unknown, flinging down science and
history in the struggle, yes, beauty herself. Did it succeed? Books
written afterwards say "Yes". But how, if there is such an event,
can it be remembered afterwards? How can it be expressed in
anything but itself? Not only from the unbeliever are mysteries
hid, but the adept himself cannot retain them. He may think, if
he chooses, that he has been with God, but as soon as he thinks
it, it becomes history, and falls under the rules of time.'[10] It is the
kind of statement which is familiar in descriptions of mysticism.
Spirit belongs within the realm of the unsayable, and in being
objectified becomes something else.

Karl Rahner expressed a similar thought when writing about
faith as 'a letting go of oneself into the incomprehensible mystery.
Christianity is far from a clarification of the world and existence;
rather it contains the prohibition against treating any experience
or insight, however illuminating it may be, as conclusive and
intelligible in itself. Christians have less answers (at their disposal)
than other mortals to hand out with a "now everything is clear".
A Christian cannot enter God as an obvious item in the balance
sheet of his life; he can only accept him as an incomprehensible
mystery in silence and adoration, as the beginning and end of his
hope and therefore as his unique, ultimate and all-embracing
salvation.'[11]

I doubt whether Forster had this kind of theology in mind
when he wrote his essay on belief. But if he had, it might perhaps
have provided his ultimate justification for not believing in belief.
I have been concerned to make the point that belief runs risks in
becoming articulate, because in the attempt it inevitably falls short
of the experience of believing itself. In fact there can be a kind of
self-consciousness about believing which eventually undermines
belief, just as the rapid and constant repetition of a word can
render it meaningless. Believing in belief is at one remove from
the actuality of believing, in that it focuses on an attitude of mind,
a process, a system, rather than on faithful response to what can

only be received. As with idolatry, one of the most subtle roots of unbelief is the false assumption that one has managed to objectivise what cannot be objectivised, and to articulate what can only be known from within. It is like falling in love with love, enjoying the feelings and missing the person.

This presents a problem for religious institutions in that they can only convey what they hold in trust if they *do* try to objectivise and articulate. It may be that dislike of institutional religion is part of the price which has to be paid for performing this function. If so then it may be possible to look at Forster's strictures in a different light. As we have seen, he had multiple reasons for disliking organised Christianity, not all of them good ones. But the central point, that it is not articulate belief as such, but something more subtle, elusive and personal which lies at the heart of religion, may be a lesson of which Christians can usefully be reminded by his chiding. He was deluding himself, though, in imagining that it was only when threatened by war that the spiritual qualities on which he placed such value, needed what he called the stiffening effects of faith. It seems to me unarguable that without traditions of belief and communities to safeguard them, nothing of lasting spiritual value can grow or be sustained. Even the most profound spiritual insight has always had to build on the experience of others or, as someone has put it, 'to keep house in a cloud of witnesses'.

Nigel Balchin's anti-hero had an even greater dislike of the Christian community than Forster. As the waters rose about him, he could see Noah's ark floating away in the distance with its rather self-satisfied little family party on board, conscious that they alone had been chosen by God. Noah himself was very apologetic. 'I feel absolutely wretched about it. But of course the trouble was that you just don't qualify under the regulations. There it is carved in stone, and you can't get past it.'[12] Too much stiffening in fact. The trouble with traditions and communities lies in overdefinition, in the temptation to draw boundaries, when what is really needed is, to quote R. S. Thomas again, 'an unfelt pressure that, irresistible in itself [has] the character of everything but coercion'. Perhaps the right word for it is attractiveness.

So what does belief mean in practice if it is genuinely to feed the spirit, avoiding the pitfalls of fantasy and idiosyncrasy, without settling into complacency, rigidity or passive and mindless acceptance? It has been my concern throughout this book to show that there can be genuine dialogue with unbelief, and I see this as a never-ending process, vital to the health of belief itself, because to understand unbelief is in some measure to overcome it. I have deliberately not paid attention to the classic arguments for God, nor to the defence of particular doctrines. My aim has been, rather, to consider the process of believing, why belief can be difficult in our present culture and what it means to have a believing mind. That was my reason for beginning with William James and his analysis of religious experience. In contrast to this approach there is a common, but misleading, caricature of belief, one might call it the opinion poll version, which sees it as a willingness to put ticks against a list of disputed propositions. It is not that doctrinal propositions are unimportant. They are like signposts on a well-travelled road, reminders of where we might lose our way if we take no notice of them. They are guardians of the mystery, warnings against a too easy accommodation of transcendence to the limits and concepts of ordinary life.[13] A recurring aim in previous chapters has been to keep open the possibility of understanding belief in these terms, for the real substance of Christian commitment is the willingness to journey, to harness the resources of tradition to make sense of the business of living under the mercy of God.

It has to be more than an individual journey because, if the love which draws us to make the journey of faith is indeed the universal love of God, we implicitly deny it by being preoccupied with individualistic religious experience. Nor can the otherness of God be truly known without a corresponding sensitivity towards the inner depths of other people. I have referred more than once to the basic trust needed if we are to secure our own identity. It is no less needed if we are to be part of that corporate critical process I have tried to describe, whereby the tradition is constantly tested and renewed in the face of actual experience, and in the light of the real differences between those who journey together. In a word, we need the churches, despite all their faults and shortcomings. Current assumptions that it is possible to enjoy an individual spirituality, while ignoring and denigrating the bodies which, by carrying the tradition, have made individual spirituality possible, is dangerously naive. But this is not to say that the churches should fail to hear critics like Forster and Balchin who in their own way were expressing at least partially valid spiritual intuitions.

Forster can warn us against the loss of immediacy and directness, the institutionalising of what is essentially personal – and I mean personal, not individual. Balchin's unprofitable servant may have belonged to a lost generation which failed through its inability to commit itself, but at least he had grasped that in the spiritual journey there are occasions when we have to wait. His failure was not in waiting but, as he admitted, in waiting because he had always waited. There is a difference between waiting in expectancy and waiting in resignation or fear. The name of the difference is faith. In him the receptivity called for by waiting had turned into apathy.

There is a very different, and famous, example of waiting in the life of the philosopher Simone Weil. Her hesitations about being baptised into the Roman Catholic Church were not due to lack of commitment. She was passionately committed to a faith which entailed social action and sharing the sufferings of others. But she feared the narrowing effect of belonging to a social institution in which, as she put it, 'people say "we" ' – a sort of Noah's ark in fact.[14] It was not that she wanted to avoid other believers, but that she felt she would be too easily influenced by them, and that her own fierce integrity would be compromised. In her hesitancy she put her finger on the paradox of all institutional religion, that it is both necessary and dangerous – necessary because there must be an institutional bearer of tradition, and dangerous because institutions too easily become cosy, defensive and self-congratulatory. This is a further reason why the continuing critical engagement between belief and unbelief is so essential.

Simone Weil's faith was, I suspect, too intense and finely balanced to suit most people. She was at the opposite pole from those I have been considering in this chapter. She would have been incensed at the thought of giving up her search because it was all too difficult or demanding or aesthetically flawed. At the heart of her faith was passion – the passion to know, to love, to serve, to give herself at whatever cost. There is passion, too, in those religious believers whom I have criticised for presuming to know too much, many of whom likewise give themselves with extraordinary self-sacrifice. I admire the strength of their commitment, without endorsing the mental closure which many of them seem to think is required for a sufficient head of steam to be generated.

So the question I am left with at the end of this exploration of a few of the umpteen varieties of unbelief is, can one be a passionate but critical believer? Is it possible to live honestly in the confused and confusing world which the twentieth century has bequeathed to us, without losing the belief that Christ matters more than anything else in heaven or on earth? We can, of course, be repelled by, or fearful about, much that is happening in today's world, and desperately want to do something about it. But that is a merely negative reason for being passionate.

A more positive one, which encapsulates much of what I have been trying to say, is to be found in a concept used by John Milbank, albeit in a slightly different context. The concept is that of 'complex space'.[15] He illustrates it with a description of a great Gothic cathedral. One walks through such a building conscious of continually unfolding vistas. It is a whole, yet it cannot be seen as a whole. Nor, though it has been handed down to us by the past, is it ever completely finished. New spaces expressing new needs, new altars representing a multiplicity of concerns and commitments, new decorative details celebrating new ideas and discoveries, can go on being added. It is constantly decaying, and constantly being rebuilt. It can represent both diversity, and the imperfection of incompleteness, without compromising its unity or confusing its purpose. A cathedral points beyond itself. It is not defensible like a city, but open to all. Its verticality is a reminder that it is not just about human beings and human relationships. It provides a complex space which can bring home to us where, as transitory, contradictory, sinful, and yet ultimately hopeful and receptive human beings, we really stand before God.

If this is a true image of faith, then perhaps we should not be surprised at the number of people nowadays who flock to our great cathedrals. The hunger for a transcendent space within which to discover ourselves is not easily abated. There is a difference, of course, between going as tourists and going as worshippers, just as there is a difference between merely inspecting the complex space we call religion, and allowing its comprehensive and sanctified complexity to stir the spirit. Being a Christian is not primarily an intellectual exercise, and believing is not merely a matter of holding certain opinions. 'Thou hast set my feet in a large room', said the Psalmist.[16] There is passion to be found in the largeness of spirit, the huge creative energy of the Christian phenomenon at its best. The household of faith is not just 'we' over against 'them' as Simone Weil feared, but much more like a microcosm of humanity. As in a great cathedral, 2000 years of history have given us a complex space in which to experience both the simple directness of faith, and its endless richness and diversity. But we can only experience it as life-giving, rather than bewildering, in actual response to the God who surpasses knowledge, yet has shown his face to us in Jesus Christ, and in the ubiquity of whose love we are given a foretaste of the many mansions in our Father's house.[17]

Notes

Chapter 1: Belief and Unbelief

1. From the brochure for the 1998 Festival.
2. Quoted by Mark McIntosh in *Reviews in Religion and Theology* (May 1998), p. 54.
3. *The Times* (24 December 1997).
4. Peter van Inwagen, *Quam Dilecta* in *God and the Philosophers*, ed. Thomas V. Morris (Oxford University Press, 1994), p. 36.
5. Accompanying a review of John Polkinghorne's 'Belief in God in an Age of Science' in *New Scientist* (4 July 1998), p. 46.
6. John Habgood, *Confessions of a Conservative Liberal* (SPCK, 1988), pp. 7–9.
7. William James, *The Varieties of Religious Experience* (Longmans, Green and Co., 1902), p. 74.
8. ibid. p. 95.
9. ibid. p. 92.
10. ibid. p. 176.
11. Rom. 9:22–3.
12. This section owes much to Barbara Herrnstein Smith's *Belief and Resistance: Dynamics of Contemporary Intellectual Controversy* (Harvard, 1997).
13. James, op. cit., p. 348.
14. *Islam Observed*. This is an unpublished report prepared, so I was told, for the Foreign Office in 1980.
15. From a conversation with Paul Rabinow in May 1984, printed in *The Foucault Reader*, ed. Paul Rabinow (Penguin, 1991), p. 382.
16. Eph. 4:14.

17. The thought comes from R. J. Bernstein, *Beyond Objectivism and Relativism* (Blackwell, 1983), p. 12.
18. Paul Tillich, *Dynamics of Faith* (Allen and Unwin, 1957), p. 57.

Chapter 2: A Matter of Proportion

1. Richard P. Feynman, *Surely you're joking, Mr Feynman!* (Unwin, 1985), and *What do you care about what other people think?* (Unwin, 1988). A posthumously published book, transcribed from lectures, *The Meaning of It All* (The Penguin Press, 1998), was high on the best-seller lists, but is in my view disappointing. It takes 133 pages to say 'I don't know.'
2. The quotation is from Peter Atkins in Russell Stannard's *Science and Wonders* (Faber and Faber, 1996), p. 7.
3. Alexandre Koyre's *From the Closed World to the Infinite Universe* (Harper, 1958), is a classic text on this theme.
4. Blaise Pascal, *Pensées* (Everyman Edition), No. 72.
5. ibid. No. 206.
6. ibid. No. 72.
7. ibid. No. 347.
8. Martin J. S. Rudwick has explored this theme. His *Scenes from Deep Time* (University of Chicago, 1992), provides a pictorial record of ways in which the prehistoric world was imagined from the mid-eighteenth to the mid-nineteenth centuries.
9. Iris Murdoch, *Metaphysics as a Guide to Morals* (Penguin, 1993), p. 127.
10. Paul Ricoeur, *Critique and Conviction* (Polity Press, 1998), p. 169.
11. The most vociferous protagonist of the view that contingency is the be-all and end-all of evolution is Stephen Jay Gould, especially in his book *Wonderful Life* (Hutchinson, 1990). He has been criticised by Simon Conway Morris in *The Crucible of Creation* (Oxford University Press, 1998). An article, 'Replaying Life' by Kate Douglas (*New Scientist*, 13 February 1999), gives a good overview of the conflict.
12. From the Introduction to Hegel's *The Philosophy of History*. Raymond Plant's *Hegel* (Phoenix, 1997), is a helpful mini-guide to his philosophy. Charles Taylor's *Hegel and Modern Society* (Cambridge University Press, 1979) interprets him in a modern context. For a vigorous critique of Hegel's historicism see Karl Popper, *The Open Society and its Enemies* (Routledge, 1945), ch. 12.

13. I have explored this theme in a wide variety of practical contexts in John Habgood, *Faith and Uncertainty* (Darton, Longman and Todd, 1997).

Chapter 3: Explanation and Understanding

1. Both encounters have very recently been reassessed in John Brooke and Geoffrey Cantor, *Reconstructing Nature: The Engagement of Science and Religion* (T. & T. Clark, 1998).

2. Richard Rorty, quoted by R. J. Bernstein in *Beyond Objectivity and Rationalism* (Blackwell, 1983), p. 67.

3. Charles C. Gillispie, *The Edge of Objectivity* (Oxford University Press, 1960), p. 42.

4. Pietro Redondi's *Galileo: Heretic* (Allen Lane, 1988), gives a controversial account of the reasons for Galileo's condemnation, but contains much useful information about its ecclesiastical background and the wider theological issues as perceived at the time.

5. There is an interesting discussion of this whole issue in the light of the Copernican controversy in Karl Popper's essay 'Three Views concerning Human Knowledge', in *Contemporary British Philosophy*, 3rd series (Allen and Unwin, 1956).

6. In the whole of this section I am heavily indebted to Michael J. Buckley's *At the Origins of Modern Atheism* (Yale, 1987).

7. ibid. pp. 359–60.

8. Richard Dawkins in *The Blind Watchmaker* (Longman, 1986), exploits this argument to the full.

9. Buckley, op. cit. p. 331.

10. Blaise Pascal, *Pensées* (Everyman Edition), No. 555.

11. ibid. No. 555.

12. ibid. No. 585.

13. Dilthey's ideas are set in the context of a modern discussion of atheism in J. J. C. Smart and J. J. Haldane's *Atheism and Theism* (Blackwell, 1996). His influence on the German classification of the sciences is discussed in W. Pannenberg's *Theology and the Philosophy of Science* (Darton, Longman and Todd, 1976), in chapter 2 on 'The Emancipation of the Human Sciences from the Natural Sciences'. H. P. Rickman's *Wilhelm Dilthey* (Paul Elek, 1979), is an excellent introduction to Dilthey himself. I have myself expanded on the

points made in this section in the inaugural Athenaeum Lecture, *Theology and the Sciences* (1998).

14. Gadamer is the key figure here. There is a useful short discussion of his relation to Dilthey in G. Warnke's *Gadamer* (Polity Press, 1987), ch. 1. See also R. J. Bernstein, *Beyond Objectivism and Relativism* (Blackwell, 1983), part III. The phrase 'hermeneutic circle' refers to the element of circularity in all understanding. For instance, it is only possible to define the meaning of words in terms of other words. Investigation implies some foreknowledge of what to look for.

15. The issue was first brought to prominence in Peter Winch's *The Idea of a Social Science* (Routledge & Kegan Paul, 1958).

16. David Hay gives a striking example of how religious cultures could be mutually recognised during the first encounters between peoples which had probably been separated since paleolithic times, when Cortes anchored off the Mexican coast in 1519. See *Exploring Inner Space: Is God Still Possible in the Twentieth Century?* (Mowbray, 1987), ch. 1.

17. For example, by Haldane in Smart and Haldane, op. cit. pp. 121–29. Also by Keith Ward in *God, Chance and Necessity* (One World, 1996), and many others.

18. Nicholas Maxwell's *From Knowledge to Wisdom* (Blackwell, 1984) is a sustained argument to the effect that natural science has lost sight of its moral aims.

19. The phrase comes from Rowan Williams, 'Logic and Spirit in Hegel' in *Post-Secular Philosophy*, ed. by Phillip Blond (Routledge, 1998), p. 127.

Chapter 4: Moral Autonomy

1. Fyodor Dostoevsky, *The Devils* (1871). The quotation is from the Everyman Edition, vol. 1, pp. 207–8. In that translation the book was then entitled *The Possessed*.

2. Quoted in E. J. Simmons, *Dostoevsky* (John Lehmann, 1950), p. 294.

3. Friedrich Nietzsche, *The Genealogy of Morals* (1887), First Essay, Section XIV.

4. Friedrich Nietzsche, *Thus Spake Zarathustra* (1883), Introductory Discourse, para 5.

5. ibid. The Third Part, *Of Old and New Tables*, para 3.

6. Friedrich Nietzsche, *The Genealogy of Morals*, Second Essay, Section II.

7. Phillip Blond, *Post-Secular Philosophy* (Routledge, 1998), p. 9.

8. Quoted by Charles Taylor in *Sources of the Self* (Cambridge University Press, 1989), p. 405.

9. From his unpublished *Eric Abbott Memorial Lecture* (1996).

10. For a more extensive discussion of some of the shortcomings of the current emphasis on rights see John Habgood, 'Do too many rights make a wrong?' (*Crucible*, Church of England Board for Social Responsibility, October 1998), pp. 200–12.

11. Paul Ricoeur, *Critique and Conviction* (Polity Press, 1998), p. 100.

12. I owe this quotation to a sermon on *Marriage* by Professor Robert Rowthorn preached in King's College Chapel, May 1999.

13. The argument is discussed at some length, and from an atheistic perspective, in Robin le Poidevin, *Arguing for Atheism* (Routledge, 1996), pp. 73–86.

14. Gen. 22:1–14.

15. John Milbank, *The Word Made Strange* (Blackwell, 1997), p. 230.

16. Job 16:18–21.

17. Ps. 73:24–5 (BCP).

18. Col. 1:10; Eph. 4:1.

19. There is a brief account of such a non-religious basis for ethics in the chapter on 'Evolution and Ethics' in my book *Faith and Uncertainty* (Darton, Longman and Todd, 1997).

20. Bruno Bettleheim gives examples of this in his account of survival in a concentration camp in *The Informed Heart* (Thames and Hudson, 1960).

21. John Habgood, *Being a Person: Where Faith and Science Meet* (Hodder and Stoughton, 1998).

22. William James, *The Varieties of Religious Experience* (Longmans, Green and Co., 1902), p. 329ff, gives examples of ways in which ideas of God have been discredited by changed moral perceptions.

23. The need for children to grow up in a secure and disciplined environment has become increasingly evident as the alternatives have been tried. Hence perhaps the popularity of a recently published book for potential parents with the title, *Saying No* by Asha Phillips (Faber and Faber, 1999).

24. Quoted by Camille Paglia in *Sexual Personae* (Penguin, 1990), p. 567.

25. Sartre, *Huis clos*, scene v.
26. George Steiner, *No Passion Spent* (Faber and Faber, 1996), p. 341.
27. Lieven Boeve, 'Market and Religion in Postmodern Culture' in *Theology* (1999), vol. CII, pp. 28–36.
28. Gwendolen Greene, *Letters of Baron von Hugel to a Niece* (J. M. Dent, 1928), XXIX.
29. Ps. 119:54.
30. Taylor, op. cit. pp. 410–13.
31. 1 John 4:19 (adapted).

Chapter 5: All or None

1. *Augustus Carp Esq. by Himself* (Heinemann, 1966), pp. 249–50. The book first appeared anonymously in 1924, but was then almost forgotten. It was revived in 1966 with an introduction by Anthony Burgess, and its author was revealed as Sir Henry Bashford, Chief Medical Officer to the Post Office and Honorary Physician to King George VI.
2. William James, *The Varieties of Religious Experience* (Longmans, Green and Co., 1902), pp. 487–88.
3. ibid. p. 517.
4. ibid. p. 514.
5. From an interview with Michel Foucault in *The Foucault Reader*, ed. by Paul Rabinow (Penguin, 1986), p. 73.
6. Sherry Turkle, *Life on the Screen: Identity in the Age of the Internet* (Weidenfield and Nicholson, 1995), p. 257. The book contains many examples of the so-called Multi-User Domains – fantasy worlds created on the Internet by players who relate to one another using assumed characters. The matters discussed in this paragraph are considered at greater length in John Habgood, *Being a Person: Where Faith and Science Meet* (Hodder and Stoughton, 1998), ch. 6.
7. Kenneth J. Gergen, *Realities and Relationship: Soundings in Social Construction* (Harvard University Press, 1994), p. 108.
8. Paul Tillich, *The Courage to Be* (Nisbet, 1952).
9. Anthony Giddens, *Modernity and Self-Identity* (Polity Press, 1991), p. 88ff.
10. ibid. p. 187.
11. Extracts from Evans-Pritchard's *Witchcraft among the Azande* (1929), and some of the criticisms of it, are conveniently brought together

in Robert Bocock and Kenneth Thompson, *Religion and Ideology* (Manchester University Press, 1985), pp. 84–123. Richard J. Bernstein, *Beyond Objectivism and Relativism* (Blackwell, 1983), also contains a discussion of the Azande on pp. 93–108.

12. Thomas S. Kuhn, *The Structure of Scientific Revolutions* (University of Chicago Press, 1962).
13. Peter Winch, *Religion and Ideology*, p. 106.
14. Alasdair MacIntyre, *Whose Justice? Which Rationality?* (Duckworth, 1988), ch. xviii.
15. ibid. p. 388.
16. There is a classic account of such dialogue, and the discoveries which can flow from it, in Klaus Klostermaier, *Hindu and Christian in Vrindaban* (SCM, 1969).
17. Akbar S. Ahmed, *Postmodernism and Islam* (Routledge, 1992), p. 93 (my italics).
18. Stanley L. Jaki, *Science and Creation* (Scottish Academic Press, 1986), p. 210.
19. This is the thesis of Fergus Kerr's *Immortal Longings* cited in Chapter 2.
20. Damian Thompson, *The End of Time: Faith and Fear in the Shadow of the Millennium* (Sinclair-Stevenson, 1996).
21. Eileen Barker, *The Making of a Moonie: Choice or Brainwashing?* (Blackwell, 1984).

Chapter 6: Anorexia Religiosa

1. George Eliot, *Middlemarch*, ch. 29.
2. From *Song of Myself*.
3. Charles Taylor, *Sources of the Self* (Cambridge University Press, 1989), p. 310.
4. Anthony Powell. The twelve volumes of the novel were published between 1951 and 1975.
5. Bryan Magee, *Confessions of a Philosopher* (Phoenix, 1997).
6. Steve Else in *Reviews in Religion and Theology* (May 1997), p. 28.
7. Heb. 10: 26–31.
8. Like Richard Dawkins.
9. Daphne Hampson, *After Christianity* (SCM, 1996), p. 245.
10. ibid. p. 25.
11. ibid. p. 38.

12. ibid. p. 139.
13. Mark 10:42–3.
14. Anthony Stevens, *Ariadne's Clue: A Guide to the Symbols of Humankind* (Allen Lane, The Penguin Press, 1998), p. 320.
15. Camille Paglia, *Sexual Personae* (Penguin, 1990), p. 3.
16. Hampson, op. cit. p. 239.
17. ibid. p. 263.
18. Anthony Freeman, *God in us. A Case for Christian Humanism* (SCM, 1993). See also Robin le Poidevin, *Arguing for Atheism* (Routledge, 1996), ch. 9.
19. Freeman, op. cit., p. 25.
20. Hampson, op. cit. p. 278.
21. Don Cupitt, *After All: Religion without Alienation* (SCM, 1994), p. 7.
22. ibid. p. 49.
23. Bryan Magee, op. cit. has much to say about experience being prior to words. See pp. 95ff.
24. M. A. Arbib and M. Hesse, *The Construction of Reality* (Cambridge University Press, 1986), p. 243.

Chapter 7: The Presence of an Absence

1. Pascal Boyer, *The Naturalness of Religious Ideas: A Cognitive Theory of Religion* (University of California Press, 1994), cited in 2.
2. Anthony Stevens, *Ariadne's Clue: A Guide to the Symbols of Humankind* (Allen Lane, The Penguin Press, 1988), p. 171.
3. See, for example, Owen Chadwick's *The Secularization of the European Mind in the Nineteenth Century* (Cambridge University Press, 1975). A. N. Wilson's *God's Funeral* (John Murray, 1999), is the most recent example of the genre.
4. Ps. 44:25.
5. Ps. 80:3.
6. Ps. 88:14.
7. Ps. 89:46.
8. Exod. 33:23.
9. Jer. 18:17.
10. I owe much of this section to an article by William Poteat on 'The Absence of God', in the *Hibbert Journal* (January 1957), pp. 115–23.
11. Blaise Pascal, *Pensées*, No. 585.
12. Unless otherwise stated, all the poems quoted in notes 12–20 are to

be found in R. S. Thomas, *Later Poems 1972–1982* (Macmillan, 1983). 'Via Negativa' is on p. 23. There is an excellent chapter on 'God Absent and Present' in J. P. Ward, *The Poetry of R. S. Thomas* (Poetry Wales Press, 1987).

13. 'The Absence' p. 123.

14. 'Pilgrimages' p. 125.

15. 'Emerging' p. 117.

16. This is an important theme in Charles Taylor, *Sources of the Self* (Cambridge University Press, 1989), especially Ch. 2.

17. 'Perhaps' p. 115.

18. 'Suddenly' from R. S. Thomas, *Frequencies* (Macmillan, 1978).

19. 'Countering' from R. S. Thomas, *Experimenting with an Amen* (Macmillan, 1986).

20. 'Gradual' p. 178.

21. William James, *The Varieties of Religious Experience* (Longmans, Green and Co., 1902), p. 517.

22. Richard Worsley, 'Savage Mystery of the Universe' in *Theology*, (November 1993), p. 451.

23. Jürgen Moltmann, *God in Creation. An Ecological Doctrine of Creation* (SCM, 1985), pp. 87–93. I am conscious that the theology expressed in these few quotations is absurdly inadequate in view of the magnitude of the subject. My excuse is that there are already innumerable books on the problem of evil and suffering, and that to pursue the subject in any detail would take me too far from my main themes. One of the best of them, in my view, is by Paul S. Fiddes, *The Creative Suffering of God* (Oxford University Press, 1988).

24. M. M. Waldorp, *Complexity: The Emerging Science at the Edge of Order and Chaos* (Penguin, 1992).

Chapter 8: Believing in Belief

1. E. M. Forster, *Two Cheers for Democracy* (Edward Arnold, 1951), p. 77.

2. Nigel Balchin, *Lord, I was Afraid* (Collins, 1947), p. 320.

3. *Sunday Telegraph Magazine* (24 August 1997). I have elaborated the general point in a lecture 'A Mirror of Eternity', reprinted in *Seeing Ourselves*, ed. Stephen Platten (Canterbury Press, 1998). The growing unwillingness of many couples to commit themselves in marriage is a further example of the same syndrome.

4. Exodus 23:19.
5. Peter van Inwagen in his essay, *Quam Dilecta*, in *God and the Philosophers*, ed. Thomas V. Morris (Oxford University Press, 1994), p. 44.
6. David Hay, *Religious Experience Today: Studying the Facts* (Mowbray, 1990). Grace Davie, *Religion in Britain since 1945: Believing without Belonging* (Blackwell, 1994), is also relevant to the concept of unrooted and inarticulate religion.
7. Monica Furlong, *Travelling In* (Hodder and Stoughton, 1971), p. 58.
8. Charles Taylor, *Sources of the Self* (Cambridge University Press, 1989), pp. 508ff.
9. *A Passage to India* (1924), ch. 11.
10. ibid. ch. 33.
11. Karl Rahner, *Theological Investigations* (Darton, Longman and Todd, 1979), vol. 16, pp. 14–15.
12. Nigel Balchin, op. cit. p. 307.
13. I have explored this theme at some length in *Being a Person* (Hodder and Stoughton, 1998).
14. Simone Weil, *Waiting on God* (Fontana, 1959), p. 22.
15. John Milbank, *The Word Made Strange* (Blackwell, 1997), p. 276. Milbank actually used the term 'complex space' in reference to the Roman Catholic Church's social teaching. But I see no reason why it should not apply equally well to belief.
16. Ps. 31:9 (BCP).
17. John 14:2 (AV).

Index